AN ILLUSTRATED HISTORY OF
ISLAM

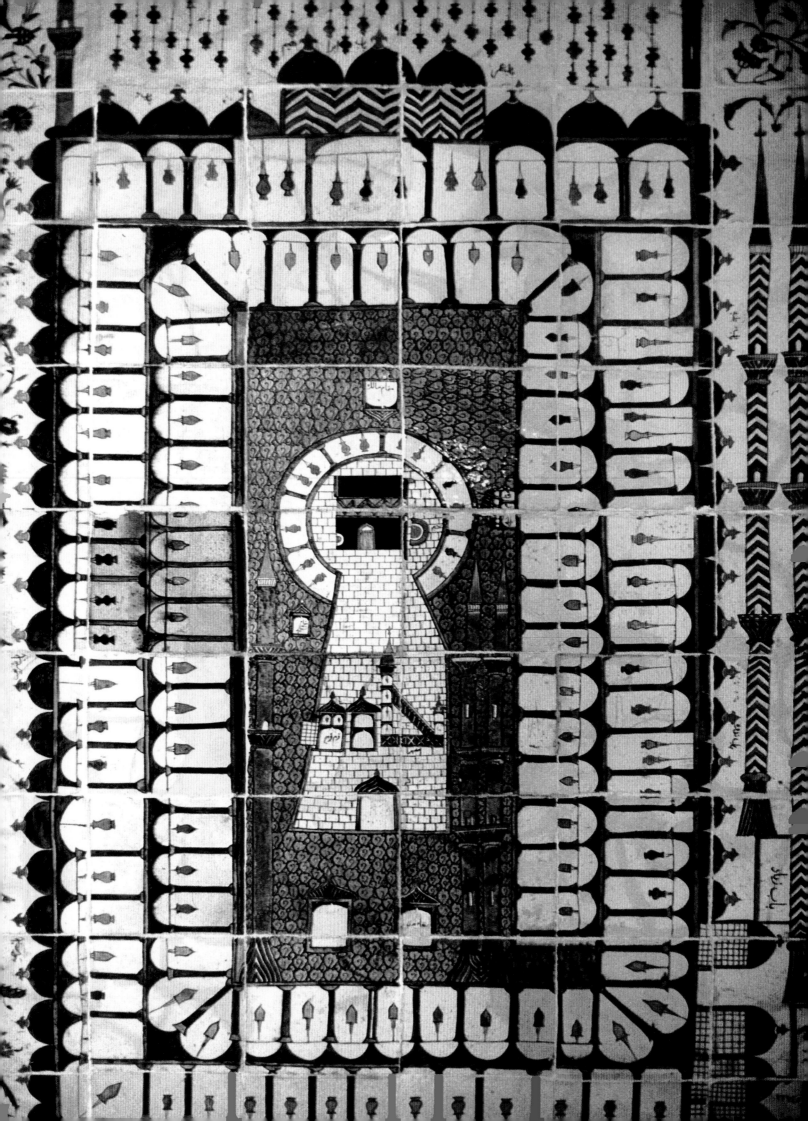

AN ILLUSTRATED HISTORY OF
ISLAM

THE STORY OF ISLAMIC RELIGION, CULTURE AND CIVILIZATION, FROM THE TIME
OF THE PROPHET TO THE MODERN DAY, SHOWN IN OVER 180 PHOTOGRAPHS

RAANA BOKHARI, DR MOHAMMAD SEDDON AND CHARLES PHILLIPS

CONSULTANT DR RIAD NOURALLAH

southwater

This edition is published by Southwater
an imprint of Anness Publishing Ltd
Blaby Road, Wigston, Leicestershire LE18 4SE
info@anness.com

www.southwaterbooks.com; www.annesspublishing.com

Anness Publishing has a new picture agency outlet
for images for publishing, promotions or advertising.
Please visit our website www.practicalpictures.com
for more information.

Publisher: Joanna Lorenz
Editorial Director: Helen Sudell
Cover Design: Nigel Partridge
Production Controller: Wendy Lawson

Produced for Anness Publishing Ltd
by Toucan Books:
Managing Editor: Ellen Dupont
Editor: Anne McDowell
Project Manager: Hannah Bowen
Designer: Ralp Pitchford
Picture Researcher: Tam Church, Mia Stewart-Wilson
Proofreader: Marion Dent
Indexer: Jackie Brind
Cartography by Cosmographics, UK

A CIP catalogue record for this book
is available from the British Library.

Previously published as part of a larger volume,
The Illustrated Encyclopedia of Islam

PUBLISHER'S NOTE
Although the information in this book is believed
to be accurate and true at the time of going to press,
neither the authors nor the publisher can accept
any legal responsibility or liability for any errors
or omissions that may have been made.

Page 1 *The Prophet's Mosque in Madinah, Saudi Arabia.*
Page 2 *Turkish ceramic tiles depicting the way to the Kaabah at Makkah.*
Page 3 *Muslims getting ready to pray at Haram Mosque, Saudi Arabia.*

Above *A candlestick from the 13th century, decorated with scenes from daily life.*

Above *An interior view of the dome in the Great Mosque of Córdoba, Spain.*

Above *The* mihrab *(arched niche) of the Tanjal Mosque, Tripoli, Lebanon.*

Above *Detail from a Persian carpet of a warrior surrounded by flowers and animals.*

CONTENTS

Above A 16th-century manuscript painting in the Mughal style.

Above 'No Conqueror But God', an inscription from the Alhambra Palace, Spain.

Above The minarets of the Sultan Hassan Mosque, Cairo, Egypt.

Above Suleyman the Magnificent, Venetian woodcut, 1540–50.

INTRODUCTION

Islam is believed to be the world's second largest religion, second to Christianity. It has more than 1.3 billion followers making up about a fifth of the global population. The meaning and message of Islam is one of peaceful submission to the will of one God, who is referred to in Arabic as 'Allah'.

Arabic is the language in which the Quran – according to Islam, a divine revelation – was disclosed to Muhammad, the 'Prophet of Islam', in 610CE in Makkah. Muslims believe that what followed over the next 23 years was a series of revelations to guide and instruct people to lead deeply spiritual, moral and upright lives, with God at the centre as sacred creator, and men and women seeking to live in peace through worship.

Above Verses from the Quran, believed by Muslims to be divine revelation, the very words of God given to Muhammad.

Below The maghrib (sunset) prayer offered at the Prophet's Mosque in Madinah, Saudi Arabia.

Within 100 years of Muhammad's death, the faith that had transformed Arabian society had extended as far as what is now Spain in the West and China in the East. The spread of Islam heralded a great time in Muslim civilization, marked by many mosques, forts and gardens that still stand today in Andalusian Spain, Moghul India and Abbasid Baghdad.

THE PROPHET OF ISLAM

Muslims consider the Quran to be the direct word of God and so do not challenge its authenticity, but a critical science of interpretation developed around the text over the centuries. Islam teaches that people cannot lead Godly lives through personal search and obedience to rules alone, but that they must depend on guidance from their

creator. This guidance, Muslims believe, came through prophets who were selected by God and sent to every nation: Adam is considered the first of these prophets and Muhammad the last.

Muhammad is central to Islam, which holds that there can be no belief in God without belief in Muhammad as his messenger. Known by Muslims as the Prophet, Muhammad is viewed not as the founder of a new religion, but rather as the restorer of monotheistic belief as practised by Ibrahim (Abraham), Moses, Jesus and others. Islam claims to be the culmination of Judaeo-Christian monotheism. The Prophet's life, as narrated in hadith (collections of the Prophet's sayings) and biographies, is the exemplary model that all Muslims aspire to follow.

ISLAM AS A WAY OF LIFE

The prescriptive and binding nature of Islam touches every aspect of life. Therefore, a Muslim's life is regulated by discipline. The five pillars of faith – declaring belief, prayers, giving alms, fasting and pilgrimage – give a ritualistic form to worship, but many Muslims believe that such observances should be imbued with inner spirituality.

Great scholarly activity after the death of Muhammad saw works in theology, philosophy, spirituality and law, as well as in the arts, sciences and medicine, being produced by independent scholars to ensure that people knew how to apply Islamic teachings to their lives.

IN THIS BOOK

Because the Prophet and his teachings are so central to Islam, this book begins with the story of the life of Muhammad, and the importance of the revelations he received, his teachings (hadith) and his life example (sunnah) to Muslim belief. It then sets out the story of the development of Islam, and the spread of Islamic civilization, beginning after the Prophet Muhammad's death and leading up to the present day.

A variety of pictures have been used to illustrate the breadth of Muslim history. Islam forbids the depiction of Muhammad in art, but Islamic history is full of vivid depictions of places and people. As it is a sensitive issue regarding the Prophet, he is generally portrayed either without facial features, veiled or surrounded by divine light.

A NOTE ON ARABIC TERMS

As Arabic is the literary language of Islam, Arabic terms have been used and explained throughout the book, and a glossary of the major words appears at the end. Spellings considered to be correct by the wider Muslim academic community have been adopted: for example 'Makkah' and 'Muslims' rather than 'Mecca' and 'Moslems'. It is customary for peace and salutations

Above Domes clustered together at the Bayezid I Mosque complex in Bursa.

to follow the names both of Islamic prophets and of Muhammad's companions, but these have been omitted in this book.

Below Pilgrims circumambulate the Kaabah in the Sacred Mosque in Makkah, the holiest site in Islam.

TIMELINE

THE FOLLOWING TIMELINE LISTS SOME OF THE MAJOR EVENTS IN ISLAM'S RICH AND CULTURALLY DIVERSE HISTORY.

- 570 Muhammad is born.
- 610 Muhammad receives his first revelation from Archangel Jibril.
- 613 Muhammad begins preaching.
- 622 Muhammad leads the *hijrah* (migration) to Madinah.
- 629 Muhammad leads a pilgrimage to Makkah, where thousands are converted to Islam.
- 630 Muhammad takes control of Makkah and rededicates the *Kaabah* shrine to Islam.
- 632 Muhammad dies.
- 632–4 Abu Bakr rules as the first caliph or successor to Muhammad.
- 634–4 Umar ibn al-Khattab rules as second caliph and calls himself *amir al-mumineen* ('Commander of the Faithful').
- 635 Muslim troops capture Damascus.
- 636 Muslims defeat the Byzantine army in the Battle of Yarmuk.
- 638 Muslim troops take Jerusalem.
- 642 A crushing victory over the Persian Sasanian army at the Battle of Nahavand delivers Persia into Muslim hands.
- 643 Muslim troops capture Alexandria in Egypt.
- 644–56 Uthman ibn-Affan rules as third caliph.
- 651 Islam is introduced to China: Muhammad's uncle Saad ibn Abi Waqqas travels as an envoy to Gaozong, emperor of Tang dynasty (618–907).
- 656 Uthman's assasination sparks civil war in the Muslim world.
- 656–60 Ali ibn Abu Talib rules as fourth caliph.
- 661 Ali ibn Abu Talib is murdered, ending the period of rule by the four 'rightly guided' caliphs.
- 661 Muawiyah I establishes the

***Above** An Ottoman manuscript depicts the first Muslims building the Prophet's Mosque in Madinah in 622.*

Umayyad caliphate (661–750).
- 680 Muawiyah's son Yazid succeeds as caliph. Ali ibn Abu Talib's son Hussein ibn Ali and followers are killed in the Battle of Karbala on 10 October.
- 711 Tariq ibn Ziyad leads the Umayyad conquest of the Iberian Peninsula. Muhammad ibn-Qasim leads the Umayyad invasion of Sindh.
- 749 Hashimiyyah rebels capture Kufa and proclaim Abu al-Abbas caliph.
- 750–1258 Abbasid caliphate.
- 756 Umayyad prince Abd al-Rahman I (reigned 756–88) establishes the emirate of Córdoba in Spain.
- 762 The second Abbasid caliph, al-Mansur (reigned 754–75), founds Baghdad as capital for the caliphate.
- 836–92 Abbasid caliphs move their capital from Baghdad to Samarra.
- 909 Ubayd Allah al-Mahdi Billah establishes Fatimid rule in Tunis.
- 929 Abd al-Rahman III (reigned 912–61) declares himself caliph of Córdoba in Spain.
- 945 Shiah Buyids take control in Baghdad, although the Abbasid caliphs remain in nominal control.
- 969 Fatimids conquer Egypt and build a royal capital at Cairo.
- 1055 Seljuk Turkish leader Toghrul Beg takes effective power in

***Above** The Dome of the Rock in Jerusalem was built in 687–92 by the fifth Umayyad caliph, Abd al-Malik.*

Baghdad. The Abbasid caliphs are still in nominal control.
- 1050 The Muslim Ghana empire in West Africa is at its height.
- 1090 Yusuf ibn Tashfin establishes Almoravid rule in Spain.
- 1099 European crusaders on the First Crusade (1096–99) capture Jerusalem from the Fatimids.
- 1100 The Christian Kingdom of Jerusalem is established.
- 1143 The Quran is translated into Latin for the first time.
- 1160s The Almohads invade Spain from North Africa and take power from the Almoravids.
- 1171 Saladin ends the Fatimid caliphate, establishing the Ayyubid dynasty (to 1250).
- 1187 Saladin recaptures Jerusalem.
- 1193 Muslim Afghan ruler Muhammad of Ghor captures Delhi, India.
- 1206 Qutb-ud-din Aybak declares himself Sultan of Delhi. Delhi sultans rule in India until 1526.
- 1212 Almohad leader Muhammad III al-Nasir is defeated by a Christian army in the Battle of Las Navas de Tolosa.
- 1236 King Ferdinand III of Castile captures Córdoba.
- 1248 Ferdinand III of Castile captures Seville.
- 1250 Izz al-Din Aybak founds the Mamluk sultanate in Egypt.
- 1258 Mongol army under Hulagu

Kahn loots Baghdad. The Abbasid caliphs take refuge in Cairo.

- 1258–1324 Osman I founds the Ottoman state in Anatolia.
- 1291 Mamluks capture Acre and drive European Christian powers from the Holy Land.
- 1327 The African Muslim Mali empire is at its height.
- 1398 Mongol ruler Timur raids Delhi. The sultanate never recovers.
- 1453 Ottoman sultan Mehmed II (reigned 1444–6 and 1451–81) captures Constantinople, renames it Istanbul and makes it the empire's capital.
- 1492 Nasrid sultan Boabdil surrenders Granada, Spain's last Muslim territory, to the Spanish monarchs Ferdinand and Isabella.
- 1502–1722 The Shiah Muslim Safavid dynasty rules Iran.
- 1517 Ottoman sultan Selim I (reigned 1512–20) defeats the Mamluk sultanate in Egypt; the final Abbasid caliph, al-Mutawakkil III, is taken to Istanbul as a prisoner. On his death, the title of caliph passes to the sultan.
- 1526 Afghan ruler Babur defeats the last Delhi sultan, Ibrahim Lodhi, and founds the Mughal dynasty.
- 1632–54 Mughal ruler Shah Jahan builds the Taj Mahal in India.
- 1740 Muhammad ibn

Abd al-Wahhab founds the Wahhabism movement. He makes an alliance with the House of Saud.
- 1744–1818 The first Saudi state dominates Arabia.
- 1824–91 The second Saudi state rules a smaller part of Arabia.
- 1839–76 In the Tanzimet period, Ottoman sultans attempt modernizing reforms.
- 1876 First Ottoman constitution is introduced but suspended in 1878.
- 1908 The revolution of Young Turks forces Sultan Abdulhamid II to abandon absolute rule and accept a constitutional monarchy.
- 1918 After the Ottoman defeat in World War I, Istanbul is occupied by British and French troops.
- 1919–23 Mustafa Kemal leads Turkish nationalists to victory in the Turkish War of Independence.
- 1923 The Republic of Turkey is proclaimed, with Mustafa Kemal Ataturk as president.
- 1924 Mustafa Kemal Ataturk abolishes the caliphate.
- 1932 The kingdom of Saudi Arabia is established by King Abdul Aziz ibn Saud.
- 1947 Pakistan is established as a Muslim-majority dominion in the Commonwealth of Nations.
- 1948 The creation of the state of Israel in Palestine.
- 1956 The kingdom of Morocco gains independence; Pakistan is

declared an Islamic republic.
- 1971 East Pakistan secedes from Pakistan to form Bangladesh.
- 1979 The Islamic Republic of Iran is established.
- 1980–8 War between Iraq and Iran.
- 1990–1 Iraqi forces invade Kuwait.
- 1991 Western-Muslim alliance drives Iraq from Kuwait.
- 1996 The Islamic fundamentalist Taliban regime comes to power in Afghanistan.
- 1998 Osama bin Laden and Ayman al-Zawahiri, leaders of the Islamic terrorist organization al-Qaeeda, issue a *fatwa* calling on Muslims to expel foreign troops and interests from Islamic lands.
- 2001 The USA declares a 'war on terror' after al-Qaeeda terrorist attacks on New York City and Washington on 11 September kill over 2,900 people. US-Western troops invade Afghanistan in search of Osama bin Laden and others, and to oust the Taliban.
- 2005 Muslim leaders and scholars from 50 countries agree the Amman Message, stating that no declarations of apostasy may be made against a Muslim.
- 2007 One of the founding members and a senior theologian of al-Qaeeda, Sayyid Imam al-Sharif, publishes a repudiation of *jihad* violence from his prison cell in Egypt.

Above Pupils flocked to learn from Persian-born polymath Ibn Sina or Avicenna (980–1037).

Above A scene from the Shahnameh *by Firdawsi (c.934–1020), who worked mostly under the Samanid rulers of Iran.*

Above Mughal Emperor of India, Shah Jahan (reigned 1628–58) built the Taj Mahal to honour his wife Mumtaz Mahal.

Arabia before Islam

UNTIL THE ADVENT OF ISLAM, ARAB CIVILIZATION HAD LITTLE IMPACT ON NEIGHBOURING ROMAN AND PERSIAN EMPIRES. THE PRE-ISLAMIC ERA WAS MARKED BY POLYTHEISM AND TYRANNY.

The city and desert dwellers of Arabia were traditionally two distinct peoples, who were shaped and conditioned by their different surroundings. Historically, the Arab Bedouins roamed the desert plains, living in territorial regions that were loosely held together by tribal codes and agreed treaties (*assabiyah*). Sedentary Arabs were originally grouped together in tribes, but in the urban setting, tribal divisions were generally social rather than geographical.

In pre-Islamic Arabia, the life of the Bedouins was romanticized by urbanized Arabs as pure, chivalrous and unrestricted. The desert Arabs were considered to embody all the noble characteristics of the Arab peoples. As a result, city children were often temporarily fostered with nomads to learn aspects of traditional Arab culture, such as the pure Arabic language, desert living, camel rearing and goat herding.

THE CITY OF MAKKAH

While the deserts of 6th-century Arabia and their inhabitants were largely overlooked by the powerful neighbouring empires of Abyssinia, Byzantium and Persia, the oasis city of Makkah was already an important Arab metropolis. It had long been established as a trading nexus between Arabia and Africa to the west, Yemen and India to the south and Egypt and Syria to the north. Trade brought wealth and status to Makkah's ruling tribes, increasing their power and influence way beyond the city.

The leading Makkan tribe of the Quraysh, the bloodline descendants of the prophet Ibrahim (Abraham),

Above The arid deserts of the Arabian Peninsula provided a breathtaking backdrop for the desert's unique people and their journey to Islam.

were the religious custodians of the ancient temple, the *Kaabah*. This square stone structure was originally built by Ibrahim, and the Quran asserts that the *Kaabah* was the first place of worship dedicated to Allah (God) (2:15–127). Elements of religious monotheism still existed in the minority communities of Jews in Yathrib (Madinah) and among

Below For thousands of years, caravans wound their way along the ancient trade routes, cutting through the oasis towns.

ORAL TRADITION

From as early as the 5th century BCE, the Arabs, originally a largely illiterate people who were proud of their tribal genealogies and histories, developed an incredibly descriptive and rhythmic language. This was achieved mostly through the custom of memorizing oral narratives from generation to generation. As the ancient nomadic cultural traditions were lost as a result of urban settlement, they were recaptured in the collective consciousness through the art of poetry and story-telling. These unique tribal narratives included genealogies of their ancestors and the extensive pedigrees of their prized camels and thoroughbred horses.

Left Bedouin Arabs socialize as they drink coffee. This is the time when they can enjoy their ancient customs of story-telling and poetry recital.

individual Arab Christians living in Makkah. However, the religion taught and practised by Ibrahim had long since been replaced by polytheism, and by the time Muhammad and his followers eventually conquered the city in 630CE, it was filled with no less than 360 statues and other images of devotion.

Below Antar, the 6th-century Arabian poet and warrior, epitomized the noble qualities of pre-Islamic desert Arabs.

BELIEFS AND SUPERSTITIONS

Polytheism prevailed in the pre-Islamic era – a period referred to in Islam as *jahiliyyah*, or 'the days of ignorance' – and every pagan Arab tribe possessed its own idol housed in the *Kaabah*. People believed that these devotional images would act as intercessors between humans and Allah (literally 'the one God'), and that by offering sacrifices and making pilgrimages to the idols they would ultimately earn God's grace and favour.

A few of the rites from the time of Ibrahim had been preserved – circumambulation, pilgrimage and animal sacrifice, for example – but they existed alongside superstitious beliefs and the worship of images. Omens, amulets, astrology and divination (by the casting of arrows) were important practices in deciding serious matters, such as when to travel, marry or go to war.

TRIBALISM AND SOCIETY

Social and tribal hierarchies also meant that the pre-Islamic period was marked by oppression, tyranny and racism. The conflicts between dissenting tribes led to continuous hostilities and strife. Slavery was a common practice, as was female infanticide, and while ownership of slaves was perceived as a sign of great wealth and power, daughters were often seen as an expensive liability. Women, whether married or not, as well as slaves were treated as personal property that could be sold or exchanged, and polygamy (the practice of marrying more than one woman) was common in pre-Islamic Arabia.

But Muhammad's prophetic call to Islam would soon transform Arabian society into a new civilization based on absolute monotheism, social egalitarianism and a fraternity of faith.

MUHAMMAD'S CHILDHOOD

WHILE MUHAMMAD WAS STILL A CHILD, AND INDEED EVEN BEFORE HE WAS BORN, THERE WERE INDICATIONS THAT THIS BOY WOULD TRANSFORM THE ARABIAN SOCIETY IN WHICH HE LIVED.

Muhammad is said to have been born in 570CE, a year that became known as the Year of the Elephant. According to a chapter of the Quran entitled 'The Elephant', Abyssinian Christians, led by army commander Abraha al-Ashram, invaded Makkah in an attempt to eradicate polytheism and destroy the ancient temple, the *Kaabah*.

Terrified, the inhabitants fled the city. But before leaving, the formal tribal shaykh (trible elder leader) Abd al-Muttalib (who was later to become Muhammad's grandfather), dared to ask the Abyssinian general to return 200 camels that had been taken from him. When Abraha expressed surprise that Abd al-Muttalib was more concerned with the camels than the religion and its shrine that he had come to destroy, Abd al-Muttalib replied, 'I am the

Above Abraha's elephants attacking the Kaabah. *This event reputedly occurred in the year of Muhammad's birth.*

lord of the camels, and the temple likewise has a lord who will defend it!' According to the Quran, the Abyssinians were miraculously bombarded by huge flocks of birds, forcing them to retreat before they could even approach the *Kaabah*.

The retreat was seen as a miracle by the Arab tribesmen, who believed they had witnessed Allah's divine intervention to protect the *Kaabah* after their abandonment of it. The Quraysh, the ancient custodians of the *Kaabah*, interpreted the attack as an omen, a precursor to a possible future event connected to the temple that had been built by Ibrahim to honour the one God.

MIRACULOUS CHILDHOOD
Later that year, Muhammad ibn Abdullah, grandson to the former tribal *shaykh* (teacher) of the Quraysh, Abd al-Muttalib, was born. Muhammad's father, Abdullah ibn Abd al-Muttalib, had unfortunately died some months earlier.

In his infancy, Muhammad was given to the care of a nursemaid, Halimah. He was fostered with her, staying with her tribe, Banu Sa'd, intermittently for the first five years of his life. The custom of foster-mothering their newborn with the Bedouins was common among the Quraysh, who wanted to imbue their children with the traditional Arab customs and pure language of the nomad Arabs.

According to a Sunni Hadith narration of Muhammad, it was during Muhammad's stay in the desert as a child that Archangel Jibril (Gabriel) came to him while he was playing with other boys. The angel allegedly held him down and split open his chest. Taking out his heart and removing a clump, he said 'this was Satan's portion of you'. He then washed Muhammad in a basin

Left During the 5th and 6th centuries, Abyssinian Christianity and civilization ruled over most of the south of the Arabian Peninsula.

Right Muhammad, cradled in his veiled mother's arms, is presented to his grandfather, Abd al-Muttalib, while the inhabitants of Makkah look on.

of gold, with water from the sacred Well of Zamzam in the *Kaabah's* precinct, before sealing his chest. The boys then ran to Halimah, shouting, 'Muhammad has been killed'. When they approached the boy, they found him pale and in a state of shock.

BAHIRA THE MONK

Muhammad's mother died when he was only six years old. The boy's paternal grandfather, Abd al-Muttalib, took charge of him, but unfortunately, he, too, died only two years later. Thereafter, Muhammad was raised by his father's younger brother, Abu Talib, a merchant and a leader of the Quraysh tribe. Muhammad benefited from the love and kindness that his uncle bestowed upon him and he would occasionally accompany him on his caravan trading trips.

When he was about 12 years old, Muhammad travelled with his uncle to Syria. Reaching the town of Busra, they met with a Christian monk called Bahira, who, unusually and for no apparent reason, insisted that they dine with him. The young Muhammad did not at first join the guests, remaining behind with the caravan's camels, perhaps to keep watch over valuable merchandise. But when Bahira saw that the boy was absent from the invited party, he asked Abu Talib to fetch him.

When Muhammad arrived, the priest immediately began to ask him a series of questions. As a result of the answers that Bahira received, he asked for permission to inspect a birthmark between Muhammad's shoulder blades. He then advised Abu Talib to take good care of his nephew, who, he declared earnestly, would become a great leader of

Right Muhammad, cradled in his veiled mother's arms, is presented to his grandfather, Abd al-Muttalib, while the inhabitants of Makkah look on.

men. Upon receiving this counsel, Muhammad's uncle concluded his business and immediately returned with his nephew to Makkah.

Although Abu Talib intuitively knew that Muhammad was special, as the Christian monk had confirmed, he could not have realized that Muhammad was, in fact, destined to become a fulfilment of Ibrahim's prophetic promise to the people of Makkah and beyond. As later asserted in the revelations of the Quran: 'and remember when Ibrahim raised the foundations of the House (*Kaabah*) with Ismail, supplicating, "Our Lord! Accept (this service) from us: for you are the All-Hearing, the All-Knowing... Our Lord send amongst them (Ismail's progeny) a messenger of their own, who will rehearse Your signs to them and and instruct them in wisdom and purify them: for You are the Exalted in Might, the Wise." ' (2:127–129)

MUHAMMAD'S IMPACT ON SOCIETY

MUHAMMAD'S EXEMPLARY CHARACTER, CARING NATURE AND WISDOM WERE RENOWNED IN THE CITY OF MAKKAH, AND HE WAS OFTEN CALLED UPON TO RESOLVE DISPUTES.

Muhammad was born into a family of noble lineage that belonged to the tribe of Banu Hashim of the Quraysh, who claimed descent from Ibrahim's son Ismail (Ismael). Pre-Islamic Arab society was based on tribal hierarchy, in which a tribe could be led to extinction in defence of its honour and that of anyone under its agreed protection.

Muhammad's family had been the ruling tribal family of Makkah at the time of his grandfather, Abd al-Muttalib. Muhammad's father, Abdullah, was the youngest and most loved son of Abd al-Muttalib but soon after marrying Aminah bint Wahb, Abdullah left with a trading caravan to Syria and never returned. The caravan came back with news of his sickness on the return journey through Yathrib (Madinah), where he eventually died. His son was born a short time later and was named 'Muhammad', meaning 'Praiseworthy', by his grieving grandfather. As Abd al-Muttalib later explained, 'I wanted Allah to praise him in heaven and mankind to praise him on earth.'

THE 'ALLIANCE OF VIRTUE'

As Muhammad reached maturity under the gentle care of his loving uncle, Abu Talib, his virtuousness earned him the title of al-Amin, 'the Trustworthy', among the inhabitants of Makkah. As a result, people would often entrust their valuables to him for safekeeping, and consult him to resolve their

Above Two Bedouin women playfully carry their children, a scene that has changed very little since the Prophet Muhammad's era.

problems and disagreements. Even as a young man, Muhammad showed commitment to issues of social justice, regardless of tribe.

A religious practice adhered to faithfully by the pagan Makkan tribes was observance of the sanctity of the month of pilgrimage, *Dhul-Hijjah*, which included a complete prohibition of hostilities. When Muhammad was 15, however, war broke out between the Quraysh and the tribe of Hawazin, which involved four years of protracted violence and bloody revenge.

The senseless bloodshed caused great loss and hardship to many people from both tribes, but as a result of their common suffering, a spirit of goodwill slowly began to prevail. Finally, another of Muhammad's uncles, al-Zubayr, took the initiative to find a

Left Pilgrims surround the Maqam Ibrahim in the al-Haram Mosque, Makkah. This shrine contains a stone that is believed to hold the permanent footprint of the prophet Ibrahim.

Above The shahadah – 'There is no God but God and Muhammad is His Messenger' – adorns the Topkapi Palace in Istanbul, Turkey.

resolution to the conflict. He called for a meeting of representatives from both tribes, in which a charitable foundation, *Hilf ul-Fudul* ('Alliance of Virtue') was established to address the needs of the needy, poor and oppressed.

Muhammad was present, and joined the foundation, stating years later, 'I witnessed an alliance with my uncles at the house of Abdullah ibn Jadan and I would not wish to exchange it for the choicest luxuries. If I were called in Islam to participate in it I would respond.'

THE BLACK STONE

On another occasion, after a flood destroyed the *Kaabah* and repairs had been completed, tribal elders were having difficulty in deciding which nobleman should replace the decorative corner piece, *al-Hajar al-Aswad*, or the 'Black Stone'. (According to tradition, this ancient relic was sent from the heavens to adorn the *Kaabah*.) As the task was one of great honour, there was much dissent. Finally, exhausted

from arguing, the elders agreed that the first person to enter the *Kaabah's* precinct would decide. When Muhammad entered, the elders were delighted, as he was renowned for his fairness and honesty. He advised them to place the stone on to a cloth to be held at each corner by a tribal elder, and he himself then placed the stone into position. Muhammad's wise and peaceful resolution to the problem averted bloodshed and united the various tribes of Makkah.

There was little doubt that Muhammad was not only a noble tribesman of great intelligence and integrity, but also that he was very generous and kind-hearted. In addition, his honesty was without question, and his ability to resolve serious problems and feuds was widely accepted. However, his rejection of the beliefs of his tribal peers, as well as his sudden claim to be an appointed prophet of God, was soon to test both the trust and the loyalties of the people of Makkah.

Right After the Kaabah *was rebuilt, arguments arose about who should have the honour of replacing the Black Stone. Muhammad's diplomacy averted tribal bloodshed.*

MUHAMMAD AND ORPHANS

Muhammad received much love and attention from his uncle Abu Talib after he was orphaned when only six years old, but he realized that the plight of most orphans did not reflect his own stable and protected upbringing and that many suffered from neglect and abuse.

Islam reflects Muhammad's concerns regarding orphans, and the Quran enshrines rights and protective measures: 'Give unto orphans their wealth. Exchange not the good for the bad (in your management thereof) nor absorb their wealth into your wealth' (4:2). And 'Come not near the property of orphans except to improve it, until he attains the age of strength (adulthood), and fulfil every agreed promise for every promise will be enquired into' (17:34).

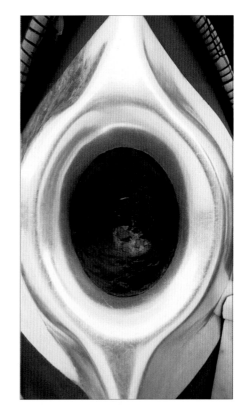

MARRIAGE TO KHADIJAH

MUHAMMAD'S WIFE, KHADIJAH, WAS A CAPTIVATING WOMAN AND 15 YEARS HIS SENIOR. SHE ENCOURAGED HER HUSBAND'S CONTEMPLATIVE LIFE AND ACCEPTED HIS MISSION AS A PROPHET.

The Quraysh tribesmen were accomplished merchants, and Muhammad's uncle Abu Talib was a wealthy businessman who encouraged his adopted nephew to become a trader. Muhammad's good character and reputation for honesty made him an ideal partner.

At the age of 25, Muhammad was employed by Khadijah bint Khuwaylid to trade for her in Syria. Khadijah was a highly successful businesswoman who employed men to work for her for an agreed percentage of the profits. After hearing of Muhammad's great honesty, she offered him a higher percentage than others in order to secure his employment. She also sent her trusted servant, Maysarah, to assist him on the long caravan.

MARRIAGE PROPOSAL

Muhammad's trading in Syria was extremely profitable, and Khadijah was pleased with both his business acumen and his outstanding moral behaviour, as observed by her servant on the trip. After discussing the matter with her close friend, Nafisah bint Munabbah, Khadijah expressed her wish to marry Muhammad, and Nafisah was asked to approach him with a proposal of marriage on her friend's behalf.

Khadijah was known for her beauty and intelligence. Many prominent men had asked for her hand in marriage, but she had consistently refused their proposals. She had been widowed and then later divorced for a number of years from her second husband, Abu Halah, and at the time of her proposal to Muhammad, she was 40 years old, some 15 years his senior.

Khadijah was a respected and wealthy woman, admired for her integrity and independence, and, like Muhammad, she was from the ruling Quraysh tribe. Muhammad willingly accepted her offer of marriage and asked his uncles, Abu Talib and Hamza, to make all the necessary wedding arrangements. As a part of the marriage dowry, Muhammad presented Khadijah with 20 pedigree camels. A modest wedding ceremony was conducted by Abu Talib at the bride's home.

MUHAMMAD'S CHILDREN

The couple lived happily until Khadijah's death at 65. His wife was a source of great comfort to Muhammad and they were blessed with two boys, al-Qasim and

Above A 14th-century manuscript painting depicts Muhammad with his wife Khadijah behind him. The third figure, on the left, is Muhammad's young cousin Ali ibn Abu Talib.

Abdullah, and according to Sunnis, with four girls, Zaynab, Ruqqaya, Umm Kulthum and Fatimah. Sadly, all Muhammad's sons died in their infancy, including Ibrahim, born to a later wife, Maria, a Coptic Christian from Egypt who later converted to Islam. Even after the death of his first-born son, al-Qasim, Muhammad was known by his *kunya* (a respectful but intimate Arab way of describing someone as 'the father of ...') Abul Qasim.

In a society that prized sons and denigrated daughters, Muhammad's loss of his male progeny became a point of ridicule among the Arabs. They mocked his prophetic mission by proclaiming, 'what we are involved in [polytheism] is more lasting than what the amputated *sunburn* [a date palm whose roots are broken] is involved in', meaning that Muhammad had no heirs to continue the propagation of Islam.

Left Ruins of the 14th-century Mosque of Fatimah, Busra, Syria. It was named for Muhammad's daughter Fatimah.

THE *HUNAFA*

Throughout his union with Khadijah, Muhammad continued the life of contemplation and seclusion that he had chosen before his marriage. He kept away from the adultery, drinking, gambling, and rivalries of pre-Islamic Makkan life and shunned the polytheism of his people. At the same time he successfully conducted his business activities and cared for the less privileged from his society.

Ibrahimic monotheism had not been completely abandoned in Arabia, and there existed a small group of people there who, like Muhammad, rejected the pervading polytheism of their tribal peers. These individuals were referred to collectively as *hunafa* (singular *hanif*), meaning 'one who follows the primordial belief in a single deity'. One such *hanif* was Zayd ibn Amr ibn Nufayl, who was known to proclaim, 'O Quraysh! By God none of you is following the religion of Ibrahim but me.'

THE REVELATION

Like Zayd, Muhammad was a *hanif*, and he would regularly visit a remote mountain cave outside Makkah to retreat in prayer and contemplation. Khadijah accepted and encouraged these retreats as a devotion that her husband had observed before their marriage.

It was during one such retreat in the month of Ramadan in 610 that Muhammad is believed to have received a visit from the Archangel Jibril, who revealed to him the first few verses of the Quran (81:22–3, 96:1–5). He returned home shaken, where he was comforted by Khadijah, who thereafter accepted her husband as a prophet. This event signalled the beginning of Muhammad's prophetic mission, the religion of Islam.

Below The 'Mountain of Light' is found on the outskirts of Makkah. Muhammad frequently made spiritual retreats on the mountain and it was here he received the first Quranic revelations.

Above Archangel Jibril is depicted in a handwritten Persian text dated to around the 14th century. According to Islamic tradition, Jibril often appeared to Muhammad in human form.

CALLED AS A PROPHET

THE QURAN RELATES THAT, FROM THE AGE OF 40, MUHAMMAD RECEIVED MANY ANGELIC VISITATIONS. THE QURAN WAS DICTATED TO HIM AND HE WAS COMMANDED TO CALL PEOPLE TO ISLAM.

Before Muhammad's call to Islam, the dominant religious beliefs and practices in Arabia were polytheistic, but there were also a number of minority groups from different monotheistic traditions.

THE MONOTHEISTS

As the religious centre of pre-Islamic Arabia, Makkah was a focus for polytheism and the *Kaabah* housed many statues and devotional images within its precincts. In contrast to the regions of Yathrib and Najran, communities of Christians and Jews were largely absent from Makkah. In this almost universally polytheistic society, they were generally prohibited from the *Kaabah* and were permitted to live – as slaves or servants – only on the outskirts of the city.

As a *hanif* (one who followed the original teachings of Ibrahim), Muhammad would have been one of the few religious monotheists living in Makkah itself. Another such man was Waraqa ibn Nawfal, a devout Christian and Khadijah's elderly cousin.

MUHAMMAD'S RETREATS

Muhammad is thought to have regularly observed spiritual retreats in a cave in the mountains on the outskirts of Makkah. Here he would spend weeks at a time in fasting, prayer and contemplation, grieving over what he saw as the erroneous religious practices and excessive lifestyles of his people. He also lamented the grave social injustices of the society in which he lived, which were often based on racial and tribal hierarchies: infant daughters were buried alive, women were traded and bartered like chattel, and slaves were treated no better than livestock.

RECEIVING REVELATIONS

According to prophetic hadith, Muhammad's many prayers and devotions to God were rewarded at the age of 40 by an unexpected angelic visitation. The story tells that Archangel Jibril appeared before Muhammad in every direction in which he gazed and that he was surrounded by a blinding light.

Above Jibril, accompanied by a group of angels, visits Muhammad. The artist has obscured Muhammad's face as a sign of respect for the Prophet.

Then, gripping Muhammad so tightly that he could barely breathe, the angel ordered him to 'Read!' Muhammad replied, 'I cannot read!' Jibril repeated the command, and on receiving the same reply, directed Muhammad to 'Read in the name of thy Lord who created, Created man from a clot, Read: and thy Lord is the Bounteous, Who teaches man with the pen, Teaches man that which he knows not' (96:1–5).

Ibn Ishaq's 8th-century biography of Muhammad, *Sirat Rasulillah*, relates that after his traumatic experience, Muhammad quickly returned home, frightened and confused. Khadijah hurriedly called for Waraqa, her Christian cousin, who, upon hearing Muhammad's encounter, concluded, 'This is the

Left Pilgrims visit the Hira cave on the 'Mountain of Light' overlooking Makkah. It was here that Muhammad is said to have received the revelations of the Quran from Archangel Jibril.

angel that God sent to Moses. I wish I were younger to witness your people exile you!' Muhammad cried 'Will they drive me out?', to which Waraqa replied, 'Anyone previously who came with something similar to what you have brought was treated with hostility: if I were to live until that day of rejection, I would strongly support you.'

THE PUBLIC CALL TO ISLAM

A lengthy period of time passed before Muhammad received further revelations, but eventually he was instructed to call his people to submit to God's will.

He began by inviting those nearest to him, starting with family and friends. After Khadijah, the first to become a declared Muslim was Ali ibn Abu Talib, the Prophet's young cousin, followed by Zayd ibn Harithah, a freed slave whom Muhammad had adopted as his son, followed by his friend Abu Bakr.

In the beginning, Muhammad's public call to Islam was merely scorned by his tribesmen, who claimed his new religion appealed only to the young, elderly and slaves. However, as the popularity of Islam spread and conversions increased, his enemies began to apply brute force and torture against its adherents.

MIGRATION TO ABYSSINIA

To relieve the oppression faced by many of his followers, Muhammad permitted a small band of Muslims to migrate to the Christian kingdom of Abyssinia. They received welcome and support from the Abyssinian King (Negus) and his subjects, despite pressure from the pagans to return them to Makkah.

They remained under the protection of the Christian king for almost two decades, living as loyal Muslim citizens, before returning to Arabia to join the burgeoning Islamic community at Madinah.

Above The Prophet Muhammad and his trusted friend Abu Bakr are depicted taking refuge from the pursuing pagans in a cave during the migration (hijrah) to Madinah.

Below Muhammad's claims to have received angelic visitations and his call to the religion of Islam provoked much discussion among the tribal leaders of the Quraysh of Makkah.

EXILE FROM MAKKAH

FEARING THAT THEIR PAGAN BELIEFS AND SOCIAL HIERARCHIES WERE
UNDER THREAT FROM ISLAM, TRIBAL ELDERS BEGAN TO PERSECUTE
AND TORTURE MUSLIMS AND TO PLOT MUHAMMAD'S ASSASSINATION.

The first exile of Muslims from the mounting hostilities of the Makkan pagans occurred around 615, when Muhammad sanctioned the migration of around 80 Muslims to Abyssinia. His public call to Islam was beginning to compromise the very fragile tribal allegiances and protection extended to him and his increasing number of followers. Muhammad's message of absolute monotheism (*tawhid*) and social equality was an anathema to the Makkan establishment.

PERSECUTION OF MUSLIMS

At the beginning of the fourth year of Muhammad's prophetic mission, the polytheists carefully aimed their persecution of Muslims at those unprotected by any tribal bonds. This meant that those already most vulnerable were targeted. When it was found that this strategy was having little impact on stemming conversions to Islam, leaders began pressuring anyone from their tribe found to be Muslim.

One of Muhammad's fiercest enemies was his uncle Abdul Uzza ibn Abd al-Muttalib, known as Abu Lahab ('the father of the flame'). Abu Jahl worked relentlessly to undermine Islam, persecuting and torturing many Muslims. A few were even killed for their beliefs.

DELEGATIONS TO ABU TALIB

In an effort to prevent conversions to Islam, a delegation of Quraysh leaders visited Muhammad's uncle Abu Talib. They complained that Muhammad was mocking their religion, cursing their gods and finding fault with their way of life. However, although Abu Talib managed to pacify the angry tribesmen, Muhammad continued to proselytize. According to Ibn Ishaq's biography of Muhammad, he told his uncle, 'if they put the sun on one hand and the moon in the other [as a reward for abandoning his mission], I would not leave it until Allah has made me victorious or I perish.'

Left Abu Jahl, Muhammad's arch-enemy, is depicted attacking the Prophet as he offers his prayers at the Kaabah.

Above A Muslim cavalryman with lance and shield rides his camel into battle, much as the Muslims would have done against the Makkan Arab pagans.

Realizing that Muhammad would not end his preaching and that Abu Talib would not forsake his nephew, Muhammad's enemies increased their oppression and torture, even plotting to kill him. On one occasion, a group led by Abu Jahl set about Muhammad while he was praying at the *Kaabah*.

When the news of Muhammad's persecution reached another of his uncles, Hamzah, an accomplished huntsman and warrior, he was so outraged that he immediately approached Abu Jahl and his accomplices. Ibn Ishaq records that, striking Abu Jahl violently across his back with his bow, he declared 'Ah! You have been abusing Muhammad: I too follow his religion and profess whatever he teaches!' The surprise conversion of Hamzah was a real blow to Muhammad's enemies.

THE YEAR OF GRIEF

A protracted series of negotiations, boycotts and plots followed in the next few years, until, in 619, Abu Talib died. Then, within a few months, Muhammad's beloved wife Khadijah passed away. These two painful events added to his trials: he had lost not only his protector but also his greatest love and spiritual companion. The pagans took advantage of this misfortune and increased their hostilities.

Muhammad is said to have suffered even greater humiliations when he visited nearby Taif to invite its people to Islam. There, the citizens set their children on him, chasing him from the city and pelting him with stones.

THE TREATY OF AQABAH

During the pilgrimage season in 621, Muhammad approached a group of pilgrims from the Khazraj tribe of Yathrib (Madinah). They were aware of the Judaeo-Christian

Below This building outside Makkah marks the site where pilgrims from Yathrib (Madinah) accepted Islam.

*Right According to Islamic tradition, Muhammad was taken on a night journey to heaven on a winged horse, al-Buraq, a year before the migration (*hijrah*) to Madinah.*

claims of a 'promised prophet' and had heard of Muhammad back in Yathrib. Muhammad explained the teachings of Islam and recited parts of the Quran to them, with the result that they were persuaded to convert to Islam.

A year later, these pilgrims returned to Makkah, along with a delegation of Muslim converts from Yathrib, and invited Muhammad and his followers to settle in their city. Muhammad ordered his followers to emigrate in small groups to avoid detection by the Quraysh, before leaving himself.

This migration, known as the *hijrah*, became a turning point for Islam. Muhammad went on to establish an Islamic community in the city, where he initiated a series of important treaties with some neighbouring tribes of both Arabs and Jews, and entered into a number of marriages with women from noble families and important tribes. The *hijrah* now marks the beginning of the Islamic calendar.

THE MADINAN COMMUNITY

THE MIGRATION (*HIJRAH*) OF MUHAMMAD AND HIS FOLLOWERS TO YATHRIB (MADINAH) TO ESCAPE PERSECUTION WAS TO BECOME PIVOTAL FOR ISLAM AND ITS SPREAD IN THE ARABIAN PENINSULA.

The persecution of Muslims in Makkah had intensified almost to the state of civil war. The two pledges that had been agreed at Aqabah between Muhammad and the Yathribite pilgrims, who had converted to Islam after their first meeting with him, became a lifeline for his prophetic mission.

Muhammad's enemies from the Quraysh were plotting a cunning assassination that would include a youth from each of the four major clans, thus avoiding any subsequent tribal bloodletting and feuding. However, when the youths attacked Muhammad's home intent on murdering him, their plot was frustrated. They found only his cousin Ali present; Muhammad had already departed from Makkah a few days earlier, and was heading for Yathrib, along with his trusted friend Abu Bakr.

Above A late 16th-century Ottoman manuscript painting shows early Muslims building the Prophet's Mosque in Madinah in 622.

ARRIVAL AT YATHRIB

After the first agreement at Aqabah, Muhammad had sent his envoy Musab ibn Umayr with the Yathribites to teach them the doctrines of their new faith and to help them propagate Islam among their fellow citizens. Musab was so successful in this mission that by the time the Yathribites returned to Makkah the following year, there was hardly a house in Yathrib without a Muslim.

The migration of many Muslims from Makkah came at considerable personal cost. Not only were most of them forsaken by their families and tribe, but their hasty exile meant that they left with virtually nothing. However, the Yathribites were generous, sharing their homes, businesses and belongings with the Muslim migrants.

Left A plan of the Prophet's Mosque in Madinah showing his pulpit, date orchard and house. It was both a religious building and political institution.

Eventually, Muhammad arrived in the city, after an eventful and dangerous journey in which he was forced to hide in a cave from the persuing Makkans. The Yathribites had been awaiting his arrival with great anticipation, and many broke out in song when they saw him on the distant horizon.

After Muhammad's migration to Yathrib, the city was renamed Madinat un-Nabi, 'City of the Prophet', in his honour.

THE ISLAMIC CITADEL

The Quranic revelations that Muhammad is believed to have received at Madinah are markedly different from those said to have been revealed to him in Makkah. While the Makkan verses concentrate on the main Quranic themes of divine unity, the coming resurrection and judgement and righteous conduct, the Madinan ones are concerned with social and political issues. These range from social relations between Muslims and others to verses communicating Shariah (divine law). Treaties and agreements between Muslims and confederate pagan-Arab and Jewish tribes are also mentioned.

These 'Madinan revelations' formed the basis of all social and political interactions and the regulating of Muslim society, state formation and Islamic dominance in the region. Muhammad was firmly established as Prophet-ruler of a virtual Islamic state within the heartlands of pagan Arabia.

Muhammad encouraged a spirit of brotherhood between the Madinite Muslims, known as *al-ansar* ('the helpers'), and the Makkan migrants, or *al-muhajiroun*, and developed a multicultural and religiously plural city-state. This was achieved by a pledge between the Christian and Jewish communities, who wished to retain their faith but pledged allegiance to Muhammad.

Right Muhammad's followers suffered a demoralizing defeat at the Battle of Uhud in 625. The prophet planned and organized his military campaigns from Madinah.

DECISIVE BATTLES

As the *ummah* began to establish itself under Muhammad's guidance at Madinah, his Makkan enemies continued in their determination to destroy Islam. This led to a number of decisive battles, some of which were won and some lost by the Muslims.

In 624, at wells of Badr near Madinah, the Muslims gained a notable victory, despite being heavily outnumbered by their opponents. However, their resilience was severly tested at Uhud, a mountain at the city boundary. In the battle here, Muslims broke their ranks, which led to a serious defeat.

Madinah was in danger of capture by 10,000 Makkans in 627 when they laid siege to the city for more than two weeks. However, the construction of a series of defensive ditches (*khandaq*) around Madinah kept the invaders at bay, eventually forcing a retreat.

BLOODLESS VICTORY

Two years after the Hudaybiyah treaty with the Makkans, which granted the Muslims permission to make pilgrimage, Muhammad marched upon Makkah with 10,000 followers. However, he did not take the city by force: instead, he granted a general amnesty. This peaceful gesture resulted in reciprocal goodwill and a mass conversion to Islam, and thus helped establish the city as the religion's spiritual centre.

Left Muhammad is flanked by angels on his triumphant return to Makkah, some eight years after the migration (hijrah) to Madinah.

ISLAM IN THE PENINSULA

BY FORGING USEFUL LINKS WITH NEIGHBOURING KINGDOMS AND TRIBES, MUHAMMAD TRANSFORMED THE ARABIAN PENINSULA WITH HIS PROPHETIC MESSAGE AND ISLAM SOON DOMINATED THE REGION.

Having established what was effectively an Islamic state at Madinah, Muhammad was able to send emissaries to surrounding tribal leaders and sovereigns. In the process he gained some important adherents, whose influence was essential to the successful long-term Islamization of the region.

TREATIES AND ALLEGIANCES

The early covenant between the Makkan Muslims and the Yathribite pilgrims at Aqabah provided an opportunity for Muhammad's message to flourish in the peninsula through the agreed migration (*hijrah*) to their city. The Yathribite tribes of Aws and Khazraj were neither Jews nor Christians, and the treaty was a useful experience for the Muslims in building alliances and propagating the doctrines of Islam to less hostile tribes in Arabia.

Once he had established Muslim ascendancy in Madinah, Muhammad quickly forged strong links with neighbouring communities. In order to accomplish his mission to promulgate Islam, it was necessary to create the right conditions for religious dialogue. To this end, Muhammad's envoys travelled to the nearby rulers of Abyssinia, Egypt, Persia, Syria and Yemen.

THE NAJRAN CHRISTIANS

Around 630, Muhammad received a delegation of some 60 Christian clergy and leaders from Najran in Yemen. They were orthodox Trinitarians who were under the protection of the Byzantium empire, and Muhammad allowed them to use the mosques to offer their Christian worship. He also took the opportunity of their visit to invite the Jews of Madinah to a tripartite religious dialogue.

During the congress, Muhammad criticized both faiths, accusing them of compromising their monotheism and tampering with their divine scriptures, thus perverting the teachings of the prophets from whom they were originally received.

Above A letter sent by the Prophet Muhammad to Chosroes II, King of Persia, inviting him to accept Islam after his defeat by the Byzantines in 629.

The Najranis acknowledged Muhammad's legitimacy as a prophet but most declined his call to Islam at that time. However, they allowed one of his companions, Abu Ubaydah ibn al-Jarrah, to accompany them to Yemen as a missionary envoy for Islam. Within a few years, the majority of Yemen, including the Christians of Najran, had converted to Islam.

THE ABYSSINIAN PRIESTS

The Christian kingdom of Abyssinia had provided asylum for a number of early Muslims, whose emigration is referred to as 'the first migration in Islam'. Relations between the Negus of Abyssinia and Muhammad were extremely cordial, to the extent that the king sent a delegation of seven priests and five monks to Madinah. They were instructed to observe Muhammad and study his revelations.

Left A Byzantine mosaic from the Umayyad Mosque, Damascus. The city came under Muslim rule in 635.

Right A mountain village mosque near Taizz. Christianity dominated Yemen until the Byzantine bishops from Najran pledged allegiance with Muhammad.

The Abyssinian clergy were visibly moved by the verses they heard and the incident was later referred to in the Quran: 'And thou wilt find the nearest in affection, to those who believe, those who say, Lo! We are Christians. That is because from amongst them are priests and monks and they are not given to arrogance.' (5:82)

In response, Muhammad sent a letter inviting the king to accept Islam. It is unclear if the Negus actually became a Muslim, but when he passed away, Muhammad announced his death and offered the congregational funeral prayer in absentia. After the 'first migration', Islam continued to flourish throughout Abyssinia.

THE JEWS OF MADINAH

Relations between the Muslims and the Jews of Madinah were at times fraught, though a large number converted to Islam. In an effort to secure peace in the city, a treaty with the remaining Jews and Christians was signed. However, although they were subject to their own religious scriptures and exempted from many duties incumbent upon Muslims, some Jews broke their agreement. They were given two options: defend against the pagan Makkans, with whom they had allied against the Muslims, or face exile. After initially refusing to do either, they left for a region called Khaybar and launched offensives against the Muslims. The consequences of this revolt were concluded at the Battle of Ahzab ('confederates') and the later Muslim offensive at Khaybar, in which the Jewish tribes and their allies were defeated.

Once the Makkans and their allies had been defeated, Muhammad turned his attention to the establishment of peace treaties with surrounding Bedouin tribes in an effort to facilitate the spread of Islam throughout the peninsula and beyond.

Left A Bedouin Muslim prays in the Sahara. Muslims used their knowledge of ancient trading caravan routes to spread Islam throughout the peninsula and into Byzantium, Persia and Africa.

MUHAMMAD'S DEATH

IN 23 YEARS, THE PROPHET MUHAMMAD HAD TOTALLY RESHAPED ARABIAN CIVILIZATION. AFTER HIS DEATH, THE CALL TO ISLAM WAS CONTINUED BY HIS MANY CONVERTS, LED BY HIS FRIEND ABU BAKR.

Although Muhammad's mission was initially met with hostility and rejection from the majority of his tribal peers, his message of Islam eventually conquered them. The new religion, which had at first been seen as a challenging and disruptive force, quickly became the dominant civilization in Arabia and beyond.

Within 23 years Muhammad was able to successfully unite Arabian society into a single community of Muslims. Islam's central creed of monotheism sparked a theological revolution across Arabia. The Arabs became religious emissaries as Islam reached far beyond the desert plains of the peninsula. Muhammad

stressed Islam's universality and egalitarianism, telling his followers: 'an Arab is no better than a non-Arab and a non-Arab is likewise no better than an Arab. A white man is no better than a black man, except in piety. Mankind are all Adam's children and Adam was created from dust.'

THE FAREWELL SERMON

Ten years after *hijrah*, Muhammad told his envoy to Yemen, Muadh ibn Jabal, 'O Muadh! You may not see me after this year. You may even pass by this very mosque of mine and my grave.' Muadh is said to have wept profusely at this news. As the *Hajj* approached, Muhammad

Above Muslim pilgrims offer their supplications as the day of prayers comes to a climax at Arafah during the Hajj. *It was here that Muhammad gave his final sermon.*

made preparations to leave for Makkah. After performing the *Hajj*, he gathered the many pilgrims on the plain of Arafah. There, he gave his final sermon, reminding them of their duty to God and that their blood and property were more inviolable than the sacredness of the *Hajj* and the city of Makkah. He then asked them all to witness that he had conveyed God's message. After they affirmed that he had, Muhammad said, 'O Allah! Bear witness'. Advising them to hold fast to the teachings of the Quran, he then concluded his sermon by receiving a divine revelation which declared: 'This day I have perfected your religion for you, completed my favour upon you, and have chosen for you Islam as your religion' (5:3).

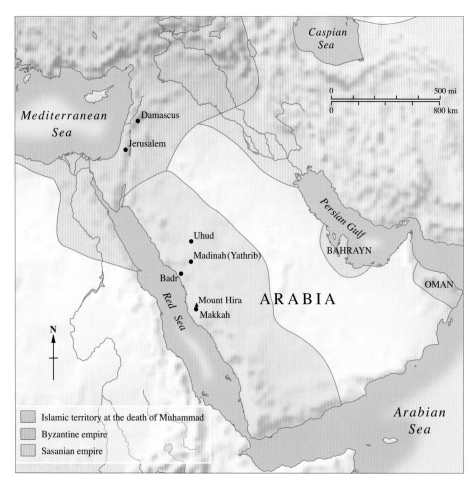

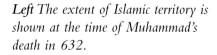

Left The extent of Islamic territory is shown at the time of Muhammad's death in 632.

MUHAMMAD'S LAST DAYS

The pilgrims understood that the *Hajj* sermon was to be the Prophet Muhammad's final address and that their beloved leader would soon depart from this world.

Soon after the *Hajj*, Muhammad became ill, and extended his yearly seclusion during the month of Ramadhan from 10 to 20 days, informing his wife Ayesha that Jibril had, unusually, revised the Quran twice with him. As he lapsed into a fever, Muhammad requested that his family repay all debts and loans. He continued to lead congregational prayers until his very last days.

On the day of his death, he is said to have gathered his family around his bed. He kissed the foreheads of his grandsons, Hasan and Hussain, and, as the pains of death gripped him, held tightly to Ayesha. Making ablutions for prayer and raising his hands, he prayed, 'O Allah! Forgive me and have mercy upon me and join me to the most exalted companionship on high.' Then he passed away.

The Madinans were stricken with grief at the news of Muhammad's death. His closest companions gathered at his house

Above Muhammad, on his deathbed, surrounded by family and companions. He was buried where he died, in his home adjacent to his mosque.

where Abu Bakr uncovered his head and tearfully kissed his face. Medieval Arab historian Ibn Hisham says that Abu Bakr then addressed the awaiting crowd, saying, 'And now, to whoever worships Muhammad, then surely Muhammad is dead. And to whoever worships Allah, then surely Allah is the Ever-living and He never dies.'

THE FIRST CALIPH

Muhammad did not appoint a successor, leaving the choice of caliph, or viceroy, to the *ummah*, or community, who convened to select their new leader. After much deliberation, it was decided that Abu Bakr was the best candidate because he was referred to by Allah in the Quran (9:40) and was said to be the most humble in prayer.

Under Abu Bakr's leadership (632–4), Islam spread into Palestine and Syria. He also established a succession of rulers, known as 'the rightly guided caliphs', from among Muhammad's companions. All three succeeding caliphs after Abu Bakr were assassinated as a result of increasing power struggles. The murdered caliphs were respected companions and relatives of the Prophet, including Ali, his cousin and son-in-law. Matters came to a head at Karbala, Iraq, in 680CE when Ali's son Hussain was killed along with his followers and family.

THE GRAVES OF PROPHETS

The Quran promises God's prophets, saints and true believers the highest positions in paradise, and most Muslims believe that, while a physical or bodily death occurs, the soul is eternal and cannot die. Prophets are believed to be not dead, but alive in their graves, existing in a spiritual domain known as *barzakh* (meaning 'a barrier between two spaces'), where they await the Day of Judgement.

Most pilgrimages to Makkah include a trip to Madinah with the specific purpose of visiting Muhammad's mosque and grave, where pilgrims offer peace and prayers to the Prophet.

Right The entrance leads to Muhammad's grave, contained within his mosque at Madinah. The site is visited by Muslims who offer prayers and blessing to the Prophet.

SEEKING KNOWLEDGE

'READ IN THE NAME OF THY LORD': THE FIRST WORDS BELIEVED TO HAVE BEEN REVEALED TO MUHAMMAD CHARACTERIZED HIS PROPHETIC MISSION TO EDUCATE AND CIVILIZE HIS SOCIETY.

Islam transformed a predominantly illiterate society into a leading civilization virtually within a single generation. The Quran provided a means of uniting diverse peoples into a single faith community, while developing their intellectual capacity through rulings that encouraged objective scientific and philosophical inquiry in the pursuit of a better understanding of Allah as al-Alim, 'the Source of all Knowledge'.

Muhammad was quite typical of his people in being an *ummi* (illiterate). The first revealed verses of the Quran are emphatic in their instruction to read and write – and thereby to seek knowledge: 'Read in the name of thy Lord who created, Created man from a clot! Read and your Lord is most Generous, Who teaches man by means of the pen, teaches Man what he does not know' (96:1–5).

SCIENCE AND LEARNING

Upon receiving this revelation, Muhammad immediately set about educating his followers to read and write. After the Battle of Badr, he decreed that any literate pagan captive who taught ten Muslims to read and write would gain freedom.

The Arabs had always used the stars to navigate their way across the deserts nocturnally. After their Islamization, they developed their knowledge of astronomy to map out the direction and times of prayers, and measure distances for travel, inventing instruments such as astrolabes, celestial globes, quadrants and sextants.

In order to obey the Quranic command to travel and experience the world that God had created, Muslims developed specific sciences that would aid exploration, and measure, analyze and quantify data and specimens. This led them to excel in the fields of science and technology.

CIVILIZATION AND CULTURE

Across the expanding Muslim world of the medieval era, from Delhi to Timbuktu and from Baghdad to Granada, Islamic culture and

Above Medieval Muslim astronomers, geographers and cartographers map out the heavens and earth, guided by the teachings of the Quran regarding natural phenomena.

learning began to advance. In Spain, the paved public footpaths of Córdoba and Seville were illuminated by street lamps. The cities incorporated public baths for the first time, and, even as early as the 9th century, underground sewers and city dumps were built to the benefit of all.

Baghdad and Cairo became the intellectual and academic centres of the Muslim world with the creation of the first universities and scientific centres, which specialized in astronomy and chemistry, philosophy and the arts.

The thirst for knowledge and the advancement in sciences and technology was not a result of market economy materialism, but rather was a living testament to the Quran's rhetorical question, 'Are those who have knowledge equal to those who do not have knowledge' (39:9)? It was also an obedient response to the Prophet

Left This 14th-century astrolabe helped Muslims to explore the universe in pursuit of knowledge of the natural world, as inspired by the Quran.

Muhammad's declaration that 'the seeking of knowledge is an obligation on every Muslim.'

Throughout the ages, Muslims have always understood the pursuit of knowledge and learning to be an act of worship that fulfils divine instructions and benefits human civilization and culture through scientific inquiry and critical thought. In no way do Muslims consider that learning results in a loss of faith or an alienation from the Islamic view of the universe.

Right The Great Mosque at Córdoba, Spain. By the 10th century, the Islamic world had become a bastion of civilization and scientific learning that stretched from Iraq right across to Spain.

PHILOSOPHY AND ART

As Muslims applied themselves to some of the more spiritual and philosophical aspects of the Quran, a number of theological disciplines emerged, including Sufism, which is often understood as Islamic mysticism. Sufism focuses on the esoteric meanings of the Quran and developed into a sophisticated branch of Islamic learning and practice. Another discipline to appear at this time was *kalam*, which is concerned with understanding the Quran through discussion of the attributes of God and theological posits on issues such as free will, sin and the nature of the Quran.

In art, the Arabesque developed an abstract and symmetrical form based on the circle and the dot, which represents God at the centre of creation. The circle and its intersecting geometric lines denote God's infinite creation as the patterns are repeated endlessly.

Left Religious devotion, geometry, acoustic sciences and skilled craftsmanship combine to produce a glorious mosque and centre of learning at the Masjid-e-Shah in Isfahan, Iran.

THE WAY OF THE PROPHET

THE QURAN TEACHES THAT THE PROPHET MUHAMMAD WAS SENT BY GOD FOR THE BENEFIT OF HUMANKIND. MUSLIMS THEREFORE BELIEVE THAT HIS LIFE EXAMPLE IS THE BEST MODEL TO EMULATE.

The Islamic declaration of faith, the *shahadah* – 'There is no God but God and Muhammad is His Messenger' – is a covenant comprised of two distinct parts. The first, 'There is no God but God', is seen by Muslims as both a negation of all false gods and an affirmation of the one true God. The second part, 'Muhammad is the messenger of God', states the Islamic belief that Muhammad is God's Prophet and that, as such, he must be obeyed and followed. Muslims believe that to obey the Prophet is to obey God, and loyalty to Muhammad's teachings and practices is therefore considered as a manifestation of belief in God.

HADITH AND SUNNAH

Islam teaches that the Prophet Muhammad is the gateway to God and that the pathway is formed of his hadith and sunnah. 'Hadith' literally means 'speech', or 'saying',

Above Reciting the Quran during Ramadhan is considered an emulation of Muhammad's ritual practice.

and refers to anything that Muhammad is thought to have said, that is the thousands of transmitted and recorded sayings of the Prophet as remembered and passed down by his early followers.

The Arabs' oral tradition and custom of memorizing genealogies, stories and poems proved invaluable in the preservation of Muhammad's hadith. A couple of generations after his death, the prophetic sayings were compiled into various hadith collections by a small number of important Islamic scholars, who also included the chain of transmitters. A transmitter is an individual who faithfully memorized a particular hadith and its chain of narrators leading to the Prophet. In Islam, the hadith collections are second only to the Quran in importance.

The word 'sunnah' refers to the life example of the Prophet. Sunnah includes Muhammad's hadith and the particular way in which he lived – the way he ate, dressed, interacted with people and performed his religious duties. Islam teaches that

Left The mihrab of the Prophet's mosque in Madinah, from where he led his congregation in prayer.

the sunnah represents the perfect life example for Muslims to follow. The accounts of Muhammad's sunnah can be found in hadith but are more commonly recorded in the biographical accounts of his life known as the *Sirah*.

EMULATING THE PROPHET

Muslims believe that Muhammad's character provides the perfect example for them to emulate in their everyday lives. The imitation of the Prophet's practices is seen as an effective way of correcting personal character traits, and in doing so, Muslims believe that they will attain God's reward.

Following the sunnah is also seen as a measure of an individual's love of the Prophet, and Muslims are particular in their appearance and conduct in an effort to faithfully imitate him. The sunnah provides a means of developing a deep spiritual bond with the Prophet.

Without Muhammad the religion of Islam could not have been realized, and Muslims believe that it is only by following his example – one seen as demonstrating love and mercy – that they are able to practise all aspects of their religious teachings. For many Muslims, love of the Prophet surpasses the love of all other humans to the point that they may become emotional at the mention of his name, to which they will often supplicate *'sallallahu alayhi wa sallam'*, meaning 'the prayers and peace of God be upon him'.

THE HADITH OF MUHAMMAD'S LAST SERMON

One of the most famous prophetic hadiths is that said to relate Muhammad's final sermon at the plains of Arafah, which he gave to his followers after his farewell pilgrimage in 632. According to this hadith, Muhammad informed his followers, 'O people listen to what I say to you for I do not know whether I will meet with you after this year in this place again…' He reminded the congregation of their duties, urging them to treat each other with kindness, then concluded by announcing to his followers, '…I have left with you that which if you hold fast to will save you from all error, a clear indication, the Book of God and the word of his prophet. O people hear my words and understand.'

Left *Muhammad delivers a sermon from his* Minbar, *or pulpit, at the Madinah mosque in this 17th-century manuscript painting.*

PRESERVING THE PROPHET'S SAYINGS

IN ISLAM, THE PROPHET'S SAYINGS ARE A SOURCE OF AUTHORITY SECOND ONLY TO THE QURAN. AUTHENTICATING WHAT MUHAMMAD ACTUALLY SAID WAS THEREFORE A PRIORITY FOR EARLY MUSLIMS.

When Muslims began to commit their religious teachings to the written word, safeguarding the authenticity and integrity of the original narrations was paramount to preserving their religion. In the process of its written compilation, the Quran was subjected to continuous scrutiny by successive caliphs and their councils. Similarly, the narrations of Muhammad needed to be collated and verified for their authenticity. Prophetic sayings are important to understanding the Quran, religious practices and legal injunctions. Preserving the correct accounts was therefore important for the development of Islamic scholarship.

BIOGRAPHIES OF THE PROPHET

The early biographies of the Prophet Muhammad are documents that capture both the critical events and developments of his mission. The works are known collectively as the *Sirah*, and the earliest is that of Muhammad ibn Ishaq ibn Yasr (d.767), who produced the book *Siratu Rasulillah (Life of the Messenger of Allah)*. These first accounts also reflect the collective memory of the Muslim community relating to the spread of Islam during Muhammad's lifetime.

Through their particular literary style, these accounts also document the love and veneration that

Right A trainee Muslim scholar learns hadith in the traditional way, at the feet of his shaykh, *or teacher, in the Islamic* madrasa *in Shiraz, Iran.*

Muhammad's first community had for him. According to ibn Ishaq, Abu Bakr's comment upon the Prophet's death was designed to affirm Muhammad's human status as compared with the eternal nature of God, who had revealed his guidance to humankind through his messenger. Abu Bakr reminded his fellow believers of God's word: 'Muhammad is but a messenger; messengers have passed away before him, will it be that when he dies or is killed, you will turn back on your heels?' (3:144) Thus Muhammad's companions were careful to avoid him becoming an object of worship in his death by focusing on the continuation of his divine mission.

However, the biography written by ibn Ishaq, while it provides details of the major events of Muhammad's life, is not more than

Above A 13th-century copy of the Quran preserves in handwritten Arabic script the original oral revelations that Muhammad is believed to have received some 600 years earlier.

a general portrait of him sketched from the shared memory of his contemporaries. Collecting the Prophet's actual hadith necessitated a more rigorous approach.

RECORDING HADITH

Two specific terms became associated with the process of writing down the Prophet's hadith: *matn*, which refers to the actual content of a hadith, and isnad, which relates to the chain of transmitters linking the Prophet to a particular hadith.

The collection of hadith gathered great momentum in the first two centuries of Islam. This was largely because the memorized accounts had been either lost with the deaths of previous generations or taken from the community at Madinah by migrating Muslims. Frequently, a hadith would find its way back to Madinah, carried by Muslims settling there who had learnt it at their place of origin from an early emigrant.

Often, early compilers would travel huge distances in order to record a single narration. For example, one scholar set out from Madinah to Damascus to seek out Abu al-Darda, a companion of Muhammad who was a transmitter of a particular hadith. The journey took a month, and necessitated some degree of discomfort, which demonstrates the extraordinary dedication of these scholars to the pursuit of religious knowledge.

THE SCIENCE OF HADITH

The collected hadiths were selected for their considered authenticity after a critical analysis of the chronological accuracy, linguistic content, geographical parameters and the character of individual transmitters connected to them.

Scrutinizing each of the links in the chain of a hadith became a biographical science called *ilm ar-rijal* (literally 'knowledge of men'). Scholars researched the reliability of character of the transmitters and also tried to establish whether linked individuals had met or if they had any political or sectarian motives. Once hadiths had satisfied the above criteria, they were classified into accepted categories of 'agreed' (or 'sound'), 'good', 'weak' or 'fabricated'.

COLLECTING HADITH

Scholars who dedicated their lives to locating and codifying hadith became known as *al-Muhaddithun*. Imam Bukhari (d.870) was one of the greatest Sunni hadith scholars and is attributed with collecting some six million hadith before accepting only 7,275 for his nine-volume work. Five other major classical volumes of hadith are still widely used throughout the Muslim world: Muslim, Tirmidhi, Ibn Majah, Abu Dawood and An-Nisai.

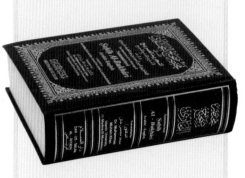

Above One of the most famous hadith collections, the nine-volume Sahih al-Bukhari *contains more than 7,000 narrations.*

Below Islamic scholars in Qom, Iran, discuss religion and memorize the Quran in the precincts of the Grand Mosque, a tradition that has endured for over a millenium.

APPLYING HADITH

A STUDY OF QURANIC TEXT AND PROPHETIC HADITH ESTABLISHED THE AUTHORITY OF A CORE OF RELIGIOUS SCHOLARS, WHO CODIFIED HADITH AND DEVELOPED THE PRINCIPLES OF ISLAMIC LAW.

By the third century after the death of Muhammad, Islamic scholarship had gravitated around a small group of specialist teachers who had devoted themselves to hadith study. These teachers also developed a system of learning, complete with a graduation. Students would study manuscripts with their master scholars, or *ulama*, either by dictation or from the original text.

CONTROVERSY

As devoted scholars of hadith worked methodically to authenticate the millions of hadiths attributed to Muhammad, other less scrupulous Muslims were engaged in their distortion and fabrication.

There were two main sources of erroneous and forged narrations. The first came from the *qussass*, or professional storytellers, who earned a living as public entertainers, relating the ancient oral narratives of the Arabs. Their tales incorporated ancient mythology, biblical legends, Quranic stories and prophetic traditions, which they fused into elaborated, entertaining plots. While the *qussass* were popular cultural communicators, the errors contained in their religious tales were often translated to the masses as fact. The result was a popular but incorrect version of many hadiths.

The second source of faulty hadiths were certain political and sectarian figures, who, for whatever reason, needed to support their claims of religious orthodoxy. In the temporary absence of a widely agreed authentic body of hadith literature, these people were able to fabricate prophetic narrations to provide justification for their various heterodox positions.

CODIFICATION

Once hadiths had been verified as genuine, it became necessary to begin codifying them into specific categories according to their

Above The imam delivers the Friday sermon to his congregation in the Grand Mosque in Almaty, Kazakhstan, praising the virtues of the Quran and hadith.

reliability and subject matter. The thematic arranging of hadith aided religious rulings relating to ritual practices and the application of Islamic law. Scholars then employed the hadith literature to explain principles of jurisprudential law known as *fiqh*.

One of the first works of this type was *al-Muwatta* (literally 'The Beaten Path') by Imam Malik (717–801). This book was followed by a number of equally important works that formed the basis of the major jurisprudential schools. Students from each of these law schools would present their own newly completed manuscripts, copied from the works of their teachers, for correction. Sometimes manuscripts would be reproduced through correspondence; others were simply copied without any supervised oral readings. Most

Left The famous university of al-Azhar, Cairo, was established in the 10th century to develop scholarship in the study of Islamic law, the Quran and hadith.

commonly, however, the scholar would provide a certificate (*ijazah*) to his student, granting him permission to transmit what he had learned.

Classical jurists, such as Imam Malik, were careful to stress that their individual opinions and rulings should not be accepted uncritically and that wherever a more appropriate ruling was available it should be preferred. Over time, the rulings of the four leading scholars, Malik, Abu Hanifah, Ash-Shafii and Ibn Hanbal, came to dominate Sunni thought, while the rulings of Imam Jafar al-Sadiq formed the leading legal school among the Shiah.

HADITH AND LAW

Islamic jurisprudence, *fiqh*, is derived from prescribed canonical laws contained in the Quran that relate to criminal and civil rulings (*muamalat*) and personal and religious commands (*ibadat*). The Quran deals with both these types of issues in broad and general terms. For example, it instructs Muslims to make ritual ablution and establish prayers, but it does not give the details of how, where and when.

The Prophet's hadith and sunnah provide precise information on these and all other matters relating to Quranic teachings. The hadith is therefore extremely important in helping Muslim scholars understand the practical application of divine laws and instructions. Had early Islamic scholars neglected to collate, authenticate and codify the hadith, the much-needed minutiae of religious law and practice would have been lost to subsequent generations of Muslims.

Right The minaret of the Oqba Mosque at Kairouan, Tunisia, which dates back to the 9th century. Its university is a bastion of Islamic learning and civilization.

HADITH COLLECTIONS

The five major collected volumes of hadith, and the special science concerned with their transmission, validation and authentication, became a distinguishing feature of Muslim civilization. The hadith collections also facilitated a unique and vast body of religious legal literature that remains available to Islamic scholars and lay Muslims.

As Muslims continue to migrate and settle into new domains, the Prophet's hadith and sunnah continue to be extremely significant

Above Students study hadith literature in the traditional manner – at the feet of their shaykh, *or teacher – in this 13th-century manuscript painting.*

in developing and establishing a functioning community, complete with its traditional values and beliefs. The wide availability of the volumes of codified hadith literature allows contemporary Islamic scholars to address new situations in accordance with the primary religious teachings of Islam.

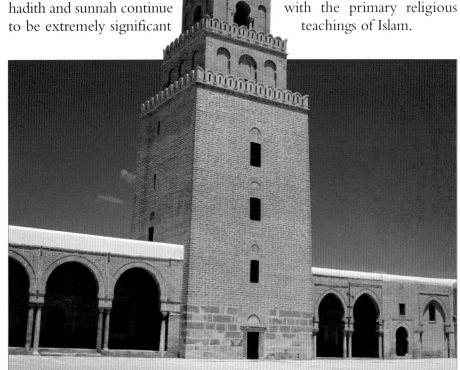

LAWS AND SCHOLARS

THE BODY OF AUTHENTICATED PROPHETIC HADITH PROVIDES THE MUSLIM *UMMAH* WITH A UNIQUE SOURCE FOR ISLAMIC SCHOLARSHIP IN THE FIELDS OF THEOLOGY AND RELIGIOUS LEGAL RULINGS.

Islamic scholarship has developed over 1,500 years through the study of the Quran and sunnah. As Islam spread beyond Arabia, the need to understand and apply its teachings in new geographical and cultural contexts grew. Muslim theologians, philosophers and legal scholars engaged in intense debates, formulating diverse theological and legal stances based on their varied interpretations of text.

ISLAMIC LAW

The laws of the Quran are called the Shariah. The method by which these rules of Shariah are applied to specific or new situations became a

science known as *fiqh*. Fiqh has four methodological principles, known collectively as *usul*: the Quran, sunnah, reasoning by analogy (*qiyas*) and consensus of opinion (*ijma*).

Fiqh scholars are known as *fuqaha* (singular *faqih*), and issues relating to legal questions are dealt with by a specialist jurist called a *mufti*, whose considered opinion is a *fatwa*. A judge dispensing with criminal and civil disputes is a *qadi* or 'grand judge'.

THE IMPORTANCE OF LEGAL SCHOOLS

Shariah is a dynamic and elaborate system that has evolved from Muhammad's time to the present. It is of major importance to the Muslim *ummah*, for whom its rules and teachings form the guiding principles and values of daily life. Although there is no notion of

***Above** An ancient Quranic manuscript handwritten in Kufic script. The Quran provides the foundations of Islamic jurisprudential law, or fiqh, through Shariah, or canonical, law.*

absolute religious authority in Islam, there is a general consensus of scholars (*ijma*) concerning the fundamental beliefs and practices. The dominant theological position within the *ummah* is referred to as *Sunni* – those who adhere to the major teachings of the Prophet and the majority opinions of the *ulama* or religious scholars.

***Below** Muslim students from Oman study the Quran, the contents and ordinances of which guide Muslims through every aspect of their daily lives.*

MAJOR ISLAMIC SCHOLARS AND SCHOOLS

During the periods of the ruling Muslim dynasties of the Umayyads and the Abbasids, *fiqh* scholarship evolved into major recognized legal schools called *madhhabs*, founded on the teachings of individual scholars. Originally there were many schools, but eventually five main ones emerged. In order of their founding, these were Hanafi, Maliki, Shafii, Hanbali and Jaafari.

The founders of these legal schools were all exceptional scholars and they share similar biographies. All spent their early lives mastering hadith literature, which they later taught. Notably, they all also resisted oppressive Umayyad and Abbasid Muslim rulers, for which most of them received public humiliation, imprisonment and even death. For example, the founder of the Hanafi School, Abu Hanifah (702–67), was born in Kufa, Iraq, and became a leading scholar in the Umayyad court, where he was offered, but declined, the position of *qadi*. Despite imprisonment, he refused another royal appointment under the Abbasid caliph al-Mansur (754–75) and thus remained in prison, where he died. Despite the fact that during their lifetimes these scholars were considered by a succession of Muslim rulers to be heterodox or heretical, their scholarship has continued to influence Muslim thought right up to the present day.

Today, the Hanafi School predominates in Turkey, Eastern Europe, Iraq, Central Asia and South Asia; the Shafii School is the main school in Yemen, Egypt, Somalia and East Asia; Muslims in North Africa and Sudan largely

Right Female law students study in a university library in Egypt. Islam has a history of women scholars specializing in religious law and jurisprudence.

follow the Maliki School; while the Hanbali school is predominant in Saudi Arabia. The main Shiah legal school, the Jaafari School, dominates Iran, Lebanon and southern Iraq.

INTERPRETATIONS

Significantly, the written script of the Quran was the first book in the Arabic language and it is the foundational text of all the various original branches of early Islamic sciences. In order to grasp the Quran's context, and thus interpret the text correctly, it is essential to understand the chronology of the Quranic revelations – the when, where, why and to whom they were given. Likewise, it is important to have an awareness of the Quran's specific language and diction, and its particular rhetorical style has been the subject of numerous detailed studies.

Above Ornately decorated copies of the Quran, some of which contain interpretations of the text, are displayed in an Islamic bookshop.

These explanatory works, which are known as *tafsir*, have three major approaches. *Tafsir bil-ra'i* gives an explanation by comprehension and logic based largely on an exegete scholar's considered interpretation of the text. *Tafsir bil-riwayah* expounds what has previously been transmitted through either other correlating verses from the Quran, specific hadiths relating to the text, or the generally agreed consensus of meaning by exegete scholars. *Tafsir bil-isharah* deals with the esoteric interpretations of the text. No individual has absolute authority on the Quran's exact meaning, but these commentaries offer a deeper knowledge of its contents.

SUCCESSORS TO THE PROPHET

THE FIRST FOUR CALIPHS – OR SUCCESSORS TO THE PROPHET
MUHAMMAD – ESTABLISHED ISLAM AS A MAJOR RELIGIOUS AND
POLITICAL FORCE IN THE MIDDLE EAST AND NORTH AFRICA.

*Above Muhammad is pictured with
the first three men to serve as caliphate
Rasulillah ('Successor to God's Prophet')
– Abu Bakr, Umar and Uthman.*

Sunnis claim that the Prophet did not name a successor before his death in 632. His followers chose Abu Bakr to be political and religious leader of the faith. Abu Bakr was named caliphate Rasulillah ('Successor to God's Prophet, Messenger of Allah'), and his rule as caliph lasted just over two years (8 June 632 until 23 August 634).

A merchant from Makkah who, like Muhammad himself, was a member of the Quraysh tribe, Abu Bakr had been a long-term companion of the Prophet, whom he had known since boyhood. He was the fourth convert to Islam, and the first outside Muhammad's own family. According to later tradition, he purchased the freedom of eight slaves who converted to the new faith in its early days.

His principal achievement was consolidating the nascent Muslim state by establishing control over the whole of Arabia. In central Arabia, his forces put down several rebel uprisings in the Ridda wars (from Arabic for 'Wars of Apostasy', and so called because a number of rebel leaders declared themselves prophets to rival Muhammad).

The most powerful rebel prophet was Musaylimah, but he and his tribe, the Banu Hanifah, were defeated at the Battle of Yamama on the plain of Aqraba (now in Saudi Arabia) in December 632. Moreover, under Abu Bakr's leadership, Bedouin tribesmen won the first of many astounding victories for the new faith against the Persian Sasanian empire and the Byzantine empire in what is now Iraq and Syria.

THE SECOND CALIPH

In August 634, Abu Bakr fell seriously ill. Before he died, he appointed Umar ibn al-Khattab to succeed him as caliph. Umar was another Makkah-born merchant and a long-term follower of Muhammad,

*Left The Prophet's daughter
Fatimah and her husband
Ali ibn Abu Talib, the fourth
caliph, witness Muhammad's
death in 632 in Madinah.*

and another member of the tribe of Quraysh. He proved a tremendously effective leader: directing operations from Madinah, in his ten-year rule (634–44) he oversaw major Islamic military expansion as his armies continued the assault against the Byzantine and Sasanian empires.

Umar's Arab armies attacked the Byzantines in Syria and captured Damascus in 635. Further south, they took control of Jerusalem from the Byzantines in 638. They also moved against the Byzantines in North Africa and took Alexandria. They seized Ctesiphon, the Persian capital, in 637, forcing the Sasanian king Yazdegerd III to flee, and vanquished the Persian army at the Battle of Nahavand in 642; in 651, Yazdegerd was killed at Merv, and the Sasanian dynasty was at an end.

To consolidate their gains, Umar's followers built garrison towns such as Kufa and Basra in Egypt. Umar was the first caliph to call himself *amir al-mumineen* ('Commander of the Faithful').

Above The Imam Ali mosque in Najaf, Iraq, contains the tomb of Ali ibn Abu Talib and is a major pilgrimage site for Shiah Muslims.

Below Ctesiphon (now in Iraq) had been a major city for 700 years when it was captured by Arab troops in 637 in the time of Caliph Umar.

UTHMAN SUCCEEDED BY ALI

In 644, Umar was stabbed in the mosque in Madinah by a Persian slave named Pirouz Nahavandi (or Abu-luluah); he died two days later. A council of elders chose Uthman ibn-Affan, − another former merchant from Makkah and another of Muhammad's original converts − as his successor, and third caliph. Some Muslims were unhappy at the choice, and dissent burst into the open after Uthman was murdered in 656.

Ali ibn Abu Talib, Muhammad's cousin and son-in-law, assumed the position of caliph and moved the capital of the Islamic community from Medina to Kufa (now in Iraq), where he had substantial support. He encountered opposition, causing the first great schism in the *ummah*.

First, he crushed a faction led by Ayesha, one of Muhammad's widows, together with Talhah and al-Zubayr, two *sahabi* ('companions of the Prophet', Muslims who were alive in the Prophet's lifetime). He defeated them decisively at the Battle of the Camel at Basra, Iraq. He also met opposition from a leading member of the Ummayad clan named Muawiyah, who refused to accept his authority.

SHIAH AND SUNNI VIEWS

Shiah Muslims regard Ali ibn Abu Talib as the first legitimate leader of the Islamic religious community by virtue of his blood relationship with the Prophet and his status as Muhammad's first convert to Islam. Entirely rejecting the authority of the first three caliphs, Shiah Muslims regard Ali as the first in a line of infallible religious leaders called imams.

Sunni Muslims, however, identify Abu Bakr and his three followers as the equally rightful successors to the Prophet in ruling the *ummah*. The Sunni celebrate Islam's first four caliphs as the *Rashidun* (the 'rightly guided caliphs'). This term and idea originated during the Abbasid caliphate (750–1258).

CIVIL WAR

THE CIVIL WAR SPARKED BY THE CLASH BETWEEN ALI AND MUAWIYAH CONTINUED INTO THE NEXT GENERATION AND LED TO THE INFAMOUS MURDER OF ALI'S SON HUSSAIN BY MUAWIYAH'S SON YAZID IN 680.

Above Ali is shown fighting the forces of Ayesha, a widow of the Prophet, at the Battle of the Camels in this 17th-century Persian wall painting.

Not long after assuming power as caliph, Ali ibn Abu Talib dismissed the regional governors appointed by his predecessors. Muawiyah, Governor of Syria, refused to obey, and proved a formidable opponent. A leading member of the Umayyad clan who had been named Governor of Syria in 640 by Umar, Muawiyah had a significant independent power base and had won major military victories, including the conquests of Cyprus in 649 and Rhodes in 654.

In response to this show of defiance, Ali led his army into Syria and fought Muawiyah in the three-day Battle of Siffin in July 657; the battle was inconclusive and the two men agreed to a six-month armistice followed by arbitration of the dispute. However, when the time came, neither man backed down and the standoff continued – with Ali as caliph and Muawiyah still defying him and acting as Governor of Syria.

Some Muslims hatched a plot to end what they saw as a damaging conflict: on the 19th day of Ramadan in 661, both Ali and Muawiyah were stabbed with poisoned swords while at prayers. Muawiyah recovered, but Ali died from his wounds two days later.

MUAWIYAH GAINS POWER

Ali's supporters named his son Hassan caliph, and Muawiyah marched against them with a vast army. The two armies fought a few inconclusive skirmishes near Sabat and subsequently, after negotiations, Hassan agreed to withdraw his claim to the caliphate. Muawiyah was at last the undisputed caliph. Under the terms of the agreement, Muawiyah was to be caliph for his lifetime. According to Sunni accounts, Muawiyah agreed that on his death, a leadership consultation (*shura*) should be held to determine the next caliph, but according to Shiah accounts, Muawiyah agreed that the caliphate would pass to Hassan's brother Hussain ibn Ali.

Below Outnumbered perhaps 500 to one, Hussain and his followers took on impossible odds at the Battle of Karbala.

Right The Imam Hussain Shrine at Karbala, close to the battlefield, contains the tombs of both Hussain and his half-brother Abbas.

Muawiyah ruled as caliph with no further challenges until his death in 680. He governed from Damascus, which he developed as a city and where he established a liberal court. His rule was notable for its tolerance towards Christians, who came to occupy many prominent government positions, and for its introduction of Byzantine-style bureaucracies, especially a postal service and chancellery. When he died, however, the terms of his agreement with Ali were ignored in his desire to found a dynasty: the caliphate was passed to his son Yazid.

EVENTS AT KARBALA

Hussain ibn Ali, brother of Hassan and grandson of Muhammad, claimed the caliphate. He marched from Makkah to Kufa in Iraq, the base of his father Ali's support. At Karbala on 10 October 680, he was intercepted by a 40,000-strong army sent by Yazid and commanded by Umar ibn Said. Hussain was vastly outnumbered, with only 72 men in his travelling party. The only survivor was Hussain's son Ali ibn Hussain, who was too sick to fight and was taken prisoner, carried off to Damascus and kept as a prisoner of Caliph Yazid. However, many years later he was freed, and in time he became the fourth Shiah imam.

The Battle of Karbala was a key cause of the centuries-long split between Sunni and Shiah Muslims. Shiahs, descendants of the supporters of Ali (their name comes from that of their party in the 7th century, the *shiat Ali*, 'the party of Ali'), do not admit the legitimacy of any of the other early caliphs nor of the Umayyad descendants of Muawiyah. Sunnis (so called because they claim to follow Muhammad's sunnah, or 'example') celebrate Abu Bakr, Umar, Uthman, Muawiyah and the Umayyads in addition to Ali as the rightful successors of Muhammad.

A SECOND CIVIL WAR

Yazid ruled, as second caliph of the fledgling Umayyad dynasty, for three years, until his sudden death in 683. He had to fight an uprising in the Hijaz region led by Abdullah ibn al-Zubayr, a member of the *sahabi* ('Companions of the Prophet'). This war is known, together with the struggle between Yazid and Hussain, as the Second Fitnah, or Islamic Civil War. Yazid captured Madinah and besieged Makkah. In the course of the fighting, the *Kaabah* was damaged, making Yazid and the Umayyad dynasty more unpopular still. Yazid's death in 683 did not bring an end to the war, which continued through the reign of the next three caliphs.

Right Around 1 million Shiah Muslims travel to Karbala each year to take part in the ceremony of Ashura that commemorates Hussain's death there.

THE POWER OF THE UMAYYADS

THE FIRST GREAT CALIPHATE DYNASTY, THE UMAYYADS, RULED THE ISLAMIC WORLD FOR 90 YEARS, FROM 660 TO 750, AND CREATED A GLITTERING CAPITAL IN THE HISTORIC SYRIAN CITY OF DAMASCUS.

Above The impressive remains near Jericho in the West Bank were once part of the Umayyads' Kirbat al-Mafjar Palace, built there in c.743–4.

The Umayyad caliphate was founded by Muawiyah I, the provincial governor who had challenged the authority of the fourth caliph, Ali ibn Abu Talib. The Umayyads took their name from Muawiyah's great-grandfather, Umayya ibn Abd Shams, and from the Banu Umayyad clan named after him. The Umayyad clan were members of the same Quaraysh tribes as the Prophet Muhammad and shared an ancestor with him – Abd Manaf ibn Qusai.

THE EARLY YEARS

Muawiyah ruled for 19 years (661–80) and established a powerful court in Damascus, Syria, but the next three caliphs of the line – Yazid, Muawiyah II and Marwan – ruled for just five years between them. The fifth Umayyad caliph, Abd al-Malik, however, imposed his authority and established the dynasty on a firm footing.

Early in his reign, Abd al-Malik defeated a rebellion in Kufa led by al-Mukhtar, who had wanted to establish another of Ali's sons, Muhammad ibn al-Hanafiyyah, as caliph. By 691, he had reimposed Umayyad authority in Iraq, and in 692, he recaptured Makkah, so ending the long-running uprising in the Hijaz; the prominent rebel, Abdullah ibn al-Zubayr, was killed in the attack.

UMAYYAD GOVERNMENT

Abd al-Malik built on the achievements of dynastic founder Muawiyah by improving and centralizing the administration of the caliphate. He introduced a new Muslim coinage with non-figurative decoration and established Arabic as the caliphate's official language.

The Arab armies and the rulers that came in their wake differed from many of their predecessors as conquerors in that they did not force people to convert to their faith. Christians, Zoroastrians and Jews were free to continue to follow their own religion so long as they paid a head tax to their new rulers. However, many conquered peoples chose to convert to Islam. Conversion was simple: the only requirement was that the new believer acknowledge formally that there is no God other than Allah and that Muhammad is his Prophet. The principal benefits were freedom from slavery – for Islam

Below The peaks of the Eastern Lebanon Mountain range rise behind the ruins of the Umayyad trading city of Anjar, which was probably built in 705–15.

guaranteed that no Muslims could be slaves – and the right to pay the lower tax that was generally levied on believers.

This financial concession, and the willingness of conquered people to convert, in fact posed a problem for the expanding empire, since the spread of conversions necessarily reduced the amount of head tax raised; there were reports of provincial governors discouraging conversions in order to protect revenue. According to traditional accounts, this problem was addressed by the Umayyad caliph Umar ibn Abd al-Aziz (717–20), a ruler revered by later generations for his wisdom, tolerance and the ascetic life he led as a ruler.

UMAYYAD DEGENERACY?
Muawiyah established – and many of his descendants maintained – a cosmopolitan court in Damascus. They appointed Syrian Christians to important administrative positions and they patronized non-Islamic artists, such as the poet al-Akhtal (640–710), who was a Christian. According to some accounts, life at court was degenerate. Not only did senior Umayyads flout Islamic law by permitting the drinking of wine, but it is claimed that one Umayyad prince even enjoyed swimming in wine. However, as tales of this kind

were circulated by the opponents of the Umayyads, there must be some doubt as to their truthfulness.

CITIES AND PALACES
The Umayyads developed the city of Damascus. Under Byzantine rule, it had been a fortress town, but the Umayyads transformed it, albeit briefly, into a great imperial city. They also built cities in the desert to facilitate the by-then flourishing international trade that made Damascus and the empire rich. One was Anjar, around 50km (31 miles) from Beirut in Lebanon, which was built by Abd al-Malik or al-Walid at the intersection of the trade routes to Damascus, Homs and Baalbek (in southern Lebanon).

Umayyad caliphs also built fine desert castles and palaces, many of which appear to date from

Above The plain exterior of the 8th-century Umayyad desert castle of Qasr Amra in Jordan conceals remarkable surviving murals depicting hunting scenes.

the brief reign of Caliph al-Walid II (743–4). Qasr Amra, in eastern Jordan, was used as a hunting lodge; its walls are covered in hunting scenes, images of fruit and naked women. Khirbat al-Mafjar, at Jericho in Palestine (c.725–50), contains a palace and bathhouse, an audience hall and a mosque. Mshatta Palace, around 30km (19 miles) south of the modern city of Amman, Jordan, was also probably built under al-Walid II; its very impressive stone façade can now be seen in the Pergamon Museum in Berlin.

Below The façade of the Umayyad Mshatta Palace, given by Ottoman sultan Abd al-Hamid II to Emperor Wilhelm II of Germany, is now in Berlin.

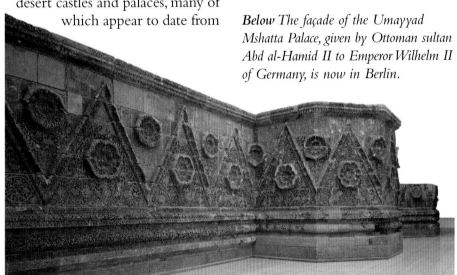

GREATER THAN ROME

BY 732, A CENTURY AFTER THE DEATH OF MUHAMMAD, THE AREA UNDER THE RULE OF THE UMAYYAD CALIPHATE WAS GREATER THAN THAT COVERED BY THE ENTIRE ROMAN EMPIRE AT ITS HEIGHT.

Above The fortified desert palace of Qasr al-Hayr al-Sharqi in Syria was built in 728–9 in the reign of Caliph Hisham (reigned 723–743).

By the beginning of the Umayyad caliphate in 661, the *Rashidun* caliphs had already taken Syria, Armenia, Egypt and most of the lands belonging to the Persian Sasanian empire. Under the Umayyads, the caliphate then expanded further east and north-east towards India and China, and far to the west and north-west across North Africa and into the Iberian Peninsula.

By 750, when the Umayyad caliphs were ousted by the Abbasids, they had created a vast empire that stretched from north-west India in the east to the Pyrenees in the north-west, and incorporated much of Central Asia, the Middle East, North Africa and what is now Portugal and Spain.

Below The army of the Goths flees before the Arab–Berber cavalry at Guadelete, in this detail from a 19th-century painting by Martinez Cubells.

EXPANSION EASTWARDS

The crushing of the Sasanian army in 642 at the Battle of Nahavand near Hamadan in Iran – a triumph celebrated by Muslims as 'the victory of victories' – delivered most of Persia into Arab hands. Afterwards, the Arabs moved on eastwards, taking Herat in 652 and Kabul in 664.

They also pressed north and north-east beyond the Persian plateau into Khorasan (an ancient region comprising parts of modern Afghanistan, Tajikstan, Uzbekistan, Turkmenistan and Iran) and Transoxiana (another ancient region in central Asia). By the early 8th century, most of this area was under Muslim control, and Arab armies pressed on still further, right to the borders of China.

After the capture of Kabul, the Indian subcontinent beckoned. The Arab armies launched attacks into the southern Punjab (in modern Pakistan) from 664 onwards. A great expedition led by Muhammad ibn-Qasim in 711 established Umayyad rule in Sindh by 712.

In one major military endeavour, however, the Umayyad armies failed. In a series of attacks in 674–8 under Caliph Muawiyah I, and again in 717–18 under Caliph Suleyman ibn Abd al-Malik, the Umayyad military machine tried and failed to capture the Byzantine capital, Constantinople.

Right A world map drawn in the 12th century by Spanish Arab geographer Abu Abdallah al-Idrisi. As is common in Islamic maps, the south is at the top.

Right A world map drawn in the 12th century by Spanish Arab geographer Abu Abdallah al-Idrisi. As is common in Islamic maps, the south is at the top.

EXPANSION WESTWARDS

Alexandria in Egypt had been taken in 643. The Arabs then pressed westwards across North Africa, taking Tripoli in 647, but met fierce resistance from the Berber peoples of the Atlas Mountains. In 670, they subdued the Berbers in building the fortress city of Kairouan (around 160km (100 miles) south of Tunis in modern Tunisia).

Once conquered, the Berbers mostly converted and joined in the expansion. Arab–Berber armies swept through the Maghreb region of north–northwest Africa, reaching Tangier (now in northern Morocco) by the early 8th century. In northern Africa, they established a Muslim territory, known to historians as Ifriqiya, which encompassed coastal regions of what is now eastern Algeria, Tunisia and western Libya. They then looked further: across the narrow Straits of Gibraltar lay the former Roman province of Hispania, ruled by the internally divided kingdom of the Visigoths.

An Arab–Berber army invaded southern Spain in 711. Berber general Tariq ibn Ziyad inspired the invaders to defeat a much larger force commanded by King Roderick of the Visigoths at the Battle of Guadalete on 19 July 711. Roderick fled, or was killed, and his kingdom was quickly taken. The invaders captured the city of Seville and swept northwards. A second army, commanded by Musa bin Nusair, Governor of Ifriqiya, arrived in 712, and the combined Umayyad forces conquered almost the entire peninsula in five years. Only in the far north did the Visigoths survive.

Umayyad forces made a number of excursions further north into southern France, but these ended in 732 at the Battle of Tours when they were defeated by Christian troops. Thereafter the Umayyads withdrew into the Iberian Peninsula, where they established the territory of al-Andalus, initially as a province of the Umayyad caliphate.

THE BATTLE OF TOURS

On 10 October 732, near Tours in France, an Islamic army of some 80,000, commanded by Abd al-Rahman al-Ghafiqi, Governor General of al-Andalus, was defeated by a Frankish–Burgundian army commanded by Charles Martel in a battle known to Muslim chroniclers as the 'Battle of the Court of Martyrs'.

Traditionally, European historians have seen this battle as a key moment in the history of the continent, when the seemingly unstoppable global progress of Islam was turned back. Certainly, after this crushing defeat, Muslims abandoned attempts at northward expansion and settled in the Iberian Peninsula, where they maintained a presence until 1492.

Right The Battle of Tours is imagined as a single combat between commanders Charles Martel and Abd al-Rahman al-Ghafiqi in this 19th-century bronze sculpture by Théodore Gechter.

TRIUMPH OF THE KILLER

IN 750, THE CALIPHATE WAS SEIZED BY THE ABBASIDS, DESCENDANTS OF MUHAMMAD'S UNCLE AL-ABBAS. THE RUTHLESS FIRST CALIPH, ABU AL-ABBAS, WAS NICKNAMED *AS-SAFFAH* ('THE KILLER').

Above Abu al-Abbas was brutal with the Umayyads, but otherwise mild in victory. He allowed Jews, Christians and Persians in his service.

The Umayyads faced recurrent opposition to their rule from Shiah Muslims, who would not allow the murder of Ali ibn Abu Talib in 661 and the slaughter of Hussain ibn Ali and family at Karbala in 680 to be forgotten.

The Abbasids, cousins of and long-term rivals to the Umayyads, began to agitate for a change in leadership. The Shiah Abassids were members of the Hashim clan, descended from the Prophet's great-grandfather Hashim through Muhammad's uncle al-Abbas. Their rebellion against the Umayyads is known as the Hashimiyyah.

THE HASHIMIYYAH

In 747, Abu Muslim became leader of the Hashimiyyah in eastern Iran. A native of the region and a convert to Islam who had become a fervently committed Shiah Muslim, Abu Muslim won the support of a group of fellow converts and non-Muslim subjects of the Umayyads to name the prominent Abassid Abu al-Abbas as a rival ruler to the Umayyad caliph Marwan II. The rebels fought under the sign of a black flag. In 749, a Hashimiyyah army captured Kufa and proclaimed Abu al-Abbas caliph there.

Marwan II attempted to put the revolt down, but on 25 January 750, an Abbasid army commanded by Abu Muslim defeated the Umayyads in the Battle of the Zab (fought on the banks of the Great Zab River, now in Iraq). Marwan escaped with his life. The Abbasids took Damascus in April 750, and in August the same year, Marwan was killed at Busir in Egypt. The struggle between the Abbasids and Umayyads is often referred to as 'the Third Islamic Civil War'.

Some Shiah clerics promoted this war as the great final conflict between good and evil prophesied for the last days of creation. They said that Abu al-Abbas was the Mahdi, or 'Redeemer', whose appearance will, according to Islamic tradition, usher in the Day of Resurrection (*yawm al-qiyamah*). Belief in the Mahdi is strong among Shiah Muslims, but generally less important to Sunni Muslims.

'THE KILLER' TAKES POWER

Abu al-Abbas established himself as caliph by ruthlessly eliminating all opposition. He invited all the leading Umayyads to a dinner at which they were all clubbed to death – all save only one. Abd

Above This silver dirham was issued by the Abbasid caliph al-Mahdi (reigned 775–85), and minted at Bukhara (now in Uzbekistan).

al-Rahman, a grandson of Caliph Hisham, escaped and fled to al-Andalus, where he forcibly removed the provincial governor of Córdoba and set himself up as Umayyad caliph, in opposition to Abu al-Abbas in Baghdad.

In Iraq, every enemy, every potential threat, was put to the sword. In their indignation, the Abbasids even despoiled all the tombs of the Umayyad caliphs in Syria, sparing only that of Umar ibn Abd al-Aziz (717–20), whose golden reputation as a wise ruler had won him the enduring respect of later generations, both Sunni and Shiah.

After establishing his family in power, Abu al-Abbas ruled for just three years, until 754. His reign is notable for the setting up of the first paper mills in the Islamic empire at Samarkand (an ancient city, now in Uzbekistan). The Arabs had learned the secret of paper making from prisoners taken in the Islamic victory at the Battle of Talas (751) against an army of the Chinese Tang dynasty.

On the death of Abu al-Abbas from smallpox in 754, the Islamic world was plunged into civil war once more: Abu al-Abbas had named his brother al-Mansur as his successor, but the latter had to fight to win power. With the support of the great general Abu Muslim, al-Mansur eventually won control of the empire; however, once established in power, he proved himself every bit as ruthless as his brother 'The Killer', ordering the execution of Abu Muslim, the man to whom the Abbasids owed their position.

UMAYYAD DOWNFALL

The Umayyads may have failed because they were so successful in secular terms. The empire expanded so extraordinarily fast, and millions of newly subject peoples converted to Islam. However, these mass conversions caused problems: the Umayyads tended to favour Arab Muslims (and particularly those of the old Arab families) over converts, and in time, the non-Arab Muslims – known as *mawali* ('clients') – grew unhappy at their treatment. This *mawali* unrest was exploited very effectively by the rebel Hashimiyyah movement that swept the Abassids to power.

Above On arriving in Spain, Abd al-Rahman, the sole survivor of Abu al-Abbas' coup, was greeted with great honour as an Umayyad prince.

Below Shiah women perform their devotions at a mosque in Baghdad, the city built by the second Abbasid caliph, al-Mansur.

The Golden Age of the Abbasids

FROM A NEW CAPITAL AT BAGHDAD, THE ABBASIDS PRESIDED OVER A FLOWERING OF ARTISTIC, SCIENTIFIC AND COMMERCIAL LIFE THAT ESTABLISHED THE EARLY YEARS OF THEIR RULE AS A 'GOLDEN AGE'.

In 762, the second Abbasid caliph, al-Mansur, built a new imperial capital called Madinat as-Salam ('City of Peace') at the village of Baghdad, beside the river Tigris in Iraq. The first Abbasid power base was at Harran (now in Turkey), but al-Mansur moved to Iraq partly to be closer to the Persian *mawali* supporters who had helped the new dynasty to power.

THE NEW CAPITAL

Al-Mansur laid out the city in the form of a circle 2.7km (1.75 miles) in diameter, with three concentric walls – and it became known as 'the

Below Al-Mutawakkil (reigned 847–61) greatly expanded the new capital at Samarra and built a splendid palace and parks beside the river Tigris there.

Round City'. At the centre stood a mosque and palace complex: four roads led outwards to the cardinal points of the compass, dividing the area within the city walls into four equal quarters, which consisted of administrative buildings and residential quarters for the caliph's guards and other members of his administration.

The city expanded outside the walls: in the area around the south gate, later known as al-Karkh, merchants built housing and bazaars. At the north-east gate, a bridge of boats led across the Tigris to the river's east bank, where the palace of the heir to the caliphate, al-Mahdi, was built.

The Abbasid capital quickly eclipsed Damascus as the trade capital of the Islamic empire. Its

Above The Mustansiriya madrasa, built from 1227–34 during the reign of the Abbasid caliph al-Mustansir, was a centre for the four schools of Sunni law.

streets were packed with craftsmen and buyers, and merchant ships from India, China and East Africa unloaded and loaded on the city's wharves. Baghdad became a city of international standing, at the height of its prosperity and fame in the late 8th and early 9th century.

Above The minaret of the Great Mosque of Samarra, built by al-Mutawakkil in c.848–52, is 52m (170ft) tall. A spiral ramp leads to the top.

PERSIAN INFLUENCE

Under the Abbasids, the Islamic world took on Persian influence; the round design of Baghdad was based on that of cities such as Ardasher-Khwarrah, or Firuzabad, in the Persian Sasanian empire. The caliphs welcomed non-Arab Muslims to their court, and many Persians rose to powerful positions in the imperial administration.

A new position of vizier, or chief administrator, was introduced, and the caliphs became more isolated from the day-to-day exercise of power, living instead in a palace amid great luxury and elaborate court ceremony, much of it derived from Sasanian models. Nevertheless, the language of the empire, spoken by caliph, courtiers and people alike, remained Arabic.

The 'golden age' of the Abbasids saw a great flowering of learning. Caliph al-Mamun founded the Bayt al-Hikmah ('House of Wisdom') as a library and centre for translation of ancient Greek, Roman, Indian and Persian works of science and philosophy, agriculture, geography, medicine, zoology and chemistry.

Yet for all their wealth and success, the Abbasids were never secure, and they faced persistent opposition. Having come to power with the support of Shiah Muslims, they had embraced Sunni Islam. Shiah Muslims living in Baghdad regularly scrawled slogans against the caliphate on the city walls, and riots in the so-called 'City of Peace' were not uncommon.

MOVE TO SAMARRA

In 836, riots engineered by the Abbasid regime's Armenian and Turkish slave soldiers persuaded Caliph al-Mutasim to move his capital to Samarra, 125km (78 miles) along the river Tigris in central Iraq. He and his successors built a beautiful palace there as well as the Great Mosque of Samarra (852); at its height the city stretched 32km (20 miles) along the banks of the Tigris. Samarra remained the Abbasid capital until 892, when Caliph al-Mutamid moved the empire's chief city back to Baghdad.

The Abbasid caliphate lasted from 750 until 1258, but for much of this period the caliphs had little real power. Beginning in the mid-900s, they became increasingly marginalized by the explosive rise of Turkish military power. They retained merely nominal authority under the rule of the Buyid and Seljuk Turks.

MATHEMATICS, MEDICINE AND ASTRONOMY

DURING THE ABBASID CALIPHATE, SCHOLARS TRANSLATED PERSIAN, GREEK AND INDIAN TEXTS TO CREATE A REMARKABLE BODY OF WORK, MOST NOTABLY IN MEDICINE, MATHEMATICS AND ASTROLOGY.

For a period, Abbasid Baghdad was the intellectual capital of the world. The vast Islamic empire brought under one ruler the descendants of several ancient civilizations of the Middle East, Asia and southern Europe for the first time since the age of Macedonian empire-builder Alexander the Great in the 4th century BCE. Frontiers were opened and Abbasids' former enemies were drawn to al-Mansur's 'City of Peace', where Greeks, Persians, Indians, Chinese, Berbers and Egyptians exchanged and compared ideas.

One of the essential features of the Abbasid 'golden age' was its tolerance. The Abbasid caliph and his administration generally promoted according to merit, and allowed Jews, Buddhists, Hindus and Christians to serve them.

THE HOUSE OF WISDOM

In 830, Caliph al-Mamun (reigned 813–33) founded the Bayt al-Hikmah ('House of Wisdom') as a library and translation centre, modelling the institution on the Imperial Library of the Sasanian Persian emperors. Authors whose works were translated include the ancient Greeks Pythagoras (*c*.580–*c*.500BCE), Hippocrates (*c*.460–*c*.377BCE), Plato (*c*.427–*c*.347BCE), Aristotle (384–322BCE) and Galen (129–*c*.216CE), and the Indians Sushruta (*c*.6th century BCE), Brahmagupta (598–*c*.665CE) and Aryabhata (476–*c*.550CE).

Now Arabic – the language in which Allah is believed by Muslims to have made his divine revelations to the Prophet Muhammad – replaced Greek as the international language of ideas.

Above Muhammad ibn Musa al-Khwarizmi's work in the House of Wisdom makes him one of the greatest figures in the history of mathematics.

MATHEMATICS

In 830, with the Byzantine emperor's permission, Caliph al-Mamun sent a delegation of scholars to Constantinople to seek classical texts for translation. Among these scholars was al-Hajjaj ibn Yusuf ibn Matar, who brought back and translated a copy of the ancient Greek mathematician Euclid's 13-volume masterpiece *Elements* (*c*.300BCE). Al-Hajjaj's successors translated from Latin a commentary on Euclid's geometry by the ancient Roman mathematician Hero of Alexandria (*c*.10–70CE) and several works by another ancient Greek mathematician, Archimedes (*c*.290–*c*.212BCE).

Perhaps the most important Islamic mathematician of the period was Muhammad ibn Musa al-Khwarizmi (*c*.780–*c*.850CE), who

Left These pages of the al-Qanun fil-Tibb (Canon of Medicine) of Ibn Sina, or Avicenna, discuss illnesses that affect the heart, stomach, skull and lungs.

Right Ibn Sina teaches medical colleagues to make remedies for smallpox in this illustration from a 17th-century Ottoman manuscript painting.

worked in the House of Wisdom under al-Mamun. Beginning in the 4th century BCE, ancient Indians had developed the figures 1, 2, 3, 4, 5, 6, 7, 8, 9 and 0 and their use in the place-value system that allows us to write any number using only these ten figures. Al-Khwarizmi learned the system through Arabic translations and explained what he called the 'Indian numbers' in his book *On Adding and Subtracting in Indian Mathematics*; this work was translated into Latin, and from it, the system he had outlined passed into European mathematics as 'Arabic numerals'.

MEDICINE

Scholars in Baghdad also made a significant contribution to later knowledge of medicine. Hunain ibn Ishaq (809–73) was a noted translator of key Greek medical works, including those of Galen and Hippocrates, and also wrote no fewer than 29 medical books of his own, including a series on ophthalmology, which were the first of the Arabic medical books to include anatomical artwork.

Two other important Islamic medical figures were the men known in the West as Rhazes and Avicenna. The first, Abu Bakr Muhammad ibn Zakariyy Razi, wrote more than 50 medical books and practised as a physician in the Iranian town of Rayy. The second, the physician and philosopher Abu Ali al-Husayn ibn Abd Allah ibn Sina (c.908–1037) wrote *The Book of Healing* and *The Canon of Medicine*.

ASTRONOMY

Encouraged by the Quran – 'And He it is Who hath set for you the stars that ye may guide your course

by them amid the darkness of the land and the sea' (6:97) – scholars in Baghdad focused on astrology and astronomy. Under Caliph al-Mamun and the direction of Sahl ibn-Harun, the House of Wisdom concentrated, in particular, on astrology and mathematics; under

Caliph al-Mutadid (reigned 892–902), another gifted translator named Thabit ibn Qurra (836–901) was appointed court astrologer. Many astronomical observatories were built throughout the empire and several navigational stars have Islamic names.

ARAB ORIGINS OF SCIENTIFIC TERMS

Several key mathematical and scientific words have their origins in Arab terms, or derive from the names of Muslim authors. The name for the mathematical discipline of algebra, for example, derives from the word *al-jabr* in the title of one of Baghdad mathematician al-Khwarizmi's books, written in *c.*825, *al-Kitab al-mukhtasar fi hisab al-jabr wa-l-muqabala* (*Overview of Calculating by Completion and Simplification*). According to one theory, 'chemistry' also has an Islamic origin, deriving from the Old Persian word *kimia* ('gold').

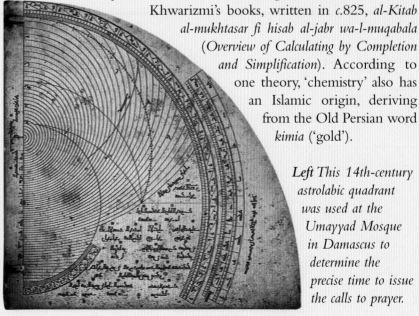

Left This 14th-century astrolabic quadrant was used at the Umayyad Mosque in Damascus to determine the precise time to issue the calls to prayer.

THE SHIAH EMPIRE OF THE FATIMIDS

FROM 909 TO 1171, THE SHIAH FATIMID CALIPHATE WAS A RIVAL POWER TO THE ABBASIDS OF BAGHDAD IN NORTHERN AFRICA AND PARTS OF THE MIDDLE EAST. IT FOUNDED CAIRO AS ITS CAPTIAL.

The Fatimids were militant Shiah Muslims who rejected the authority of the Sunni Muslim Abbasid caliphate. They were members of the mystical Ismaili sect of Shiah Islam and their rulers were Shiah imams (religious leaders). The Fatimid imams are recognized by most Muslims as holders of the office of caliph, and as a result, the period of Fatimid rule represents the only period (aside from the caliphate of Ali ibn Abu Talib) in which the caliphate and the Shiah imamate coincided.

THE FOUNDING OF THE FATIMID DYNASTY

The Fatimid dynasty was founded by Ubayd Allah al-Mahdi Billah, who claimed descent from the Prophet through Muhammad's daughter Fatimah and her husband Ali ibn Abu Talib, the first Shiah imam. Starting in Tunis in 909, al-Mahdi extended his power to cover all of the central Maghreb region (Tunisia, Libya, Algeria and Morocco), and ruled from a newly built capital at Mahdia on the Tunisian coast.

Egypt was at this time ruled by the Ikhshidid dynasty, under overall authority of the Abbasid caliph in Baghdad. The Fatimids invaded and conquered the Ikhshidids, took their capital, Fustat, and founded a new royal city in Qahirah (Cairo) in 969. Cairo became a royal enclave for the Fatimid caliph, while the administrative government of his territory was carried out from nearby Fustat.

FORCEFUL EXPANSION

At the height of the Fatmids' power in the late 10th and early 11th century, their empire included the

Above Begun by al-Aziz in 990, the al-Hakim Mosque in Cairo was finished in 1003 by al-Hakim and named after him.

whole of northern Africa, the Hejaz and Yemen, the island of Sicily and the Mediterranean coast as far north as Syria (including Palestine and Lebanon and Syria itself).

The Fatimid imams, by virtue of their descent from the Prophet, declared themselves infallible and incapable of wrongdoing, and they denounced the Abbasid caliphs as usurpers. Their aim was not simply to establish a regional power base independent of Baghdad but to supersede Abbasid power altogether to become leaders of a universal Islamic religious state. They sent missionaries throughout the Islamic world, attempting to make converts, and were a constant ideological as well as a political threat to the Sunni Abbasid caliphate.

FATIMID CAIRO

The Fatimids named their new royal enclave Qahirah after the planet Mars (then called *al-Najim al-Qahir*, 'the destroyer', or *Qahirat*

Left The beautiful al-Azhar Mosque in Cairo dates right back to the city's foundation. It was named after Fatimah az-Zahra, daughter of Muhammad.

52

al-Adaa, 'Vanquisher of foes'.) The enclave was built in 1069–73 by workers under the command of General Jawhar al-Siqilli during the reign of the Fatimid imam al-Muizz. General Jawhar himself laid the foundation stone for the splendid Mosque of Qahirah (later called al-Azhar Mosque) in 970. In 988, a *madrasa* (religious college) was established in its vicinity; this would become the prestigious al-Azhar University of Cairo.

TRADE AND GOVERNMENT

The Fatimid empire thrived on trade, particularly after an earthquake in the port of Siraf on the Persian Gulf drove traders to divert shipping into the Red Sea, close to Cairo. The empire traded in the Indian Ocean as well as the Mediterranean and established diplomatic and commercial links as far afield as the Chinese Song dynasty.

Although the Fatimids were staunch Shiah Muslims, they generally promoted to the imperial

Below Prominent Fatimids were buried in fine mausoleums in the cemetery at Aswan in southern Egypt from the 10th century onwards.

administration according to ability rather than religious orthodoxy, and Sunni Muslims, Jews and Christians all achieved high office. One major exception to this rule, however, was the eccentric and radically religious Caliph al-Hakim bi-Amrillah, (996–1021), who was violently anti-Christian and responsible for the destruction of the Church of the Holy Sepulchre in Jerusalem.

FATIMID DOWNFALL

During the last decades of the 11th century in Syria, Lebanon and Palestine, the Fatimids suffered a number of losses at the hands of the

Above These thick, sea-washed walls are remains of the 10th-century defensive fortifications at the original Fatimid capital of Mahdia on the Tunisian coast.

Buyid and Seljuk Turks and the European Christian crusaders, including that of Jerusalem to the army of the First Crusade in 1099. Their empire fell away and the Fatimids were reduced to their territory in Egypt.

During the 12th century, Fatimid power continued to wane, and they were finally defeated by Shirkuh, general of the Syrian Zangid leader Nur ad-Din, in 1169.

THE ISMAILIS

The second largest branch of Shiah Islam after the 'Twelvers', the Ismailis take their name from that of Ismail ibn Jafar (*c.*721–55), whom they recognize as the divinely chosen spiritual successor to his father, the sixth Shiah imam, Jafar al-Sadiq (702–65). (The Twelvers regard Musa al-Kazim, Ismail's younger brother, as the seventh imam.) The Ismailis follow a more mystical approach in their religion than do the more conservative Twelvers.

Buyids and Seljuks

IN THE 10TH CENTURY, THE ABBASID CALIPHS WERE OVERPOWERED BY PREVIOUSLY SUBJECT PEOPLES, AS FIRST THE IRANIAN BUYIDS AND THEN THE SELJUK TURKS TOOK CONTROL IN BAGHDAD.

Above Both Buyids and Seljuks imposed military authority on the lands of the caliphate but left the Abbasid caliphs in religious authority.

The collapse of Abbasid power began with a waning of central authority. A key development was the decision of Caliph al-Mutasim (reigned 833–42) to form an imperial bodyguard from non-Muslim Slavs, Turks and Berbers, who had been taken as prisoners of war. These bodyguards, called *ghilman*, were answerable only to the caliph. The soldiers converted to Islam, but they proved a hugely disruptive force as soon as they realized the power that lay in their hands: in the 860s, they revolted a number of times and even killed four caliphs.

The Abbasids' difficulties arose, in part, from the structures of their imperial government. With a vast empire to rule, the caliphs and their viziers, or administrators, allowed regional governors a large degree of independence, and over time, these men became increasingly autonomous and even created their own dynastic power bases.

A profusion of more or less independent dynasties – they paid only nominal respect to Baghdad – began to establish themselves. They included the Samarids of Khorasan and Transoxiana, the Hamdanids of Syria, and the Taharids, Alids and Saffarids of Iran. In North Africa, the Idrisids in the Maghreb and the Tulunids and Ikhshidids of Egypt were already effectively independent of Abbasid control by the time that the Fatimids arose in open opposition to Baghdad after 909.

BUYIDS TAKE CONTROL

The Buyids – Shiah tribesmen from western Iran – built up their power in western Iran and Iraq in the years after *c.*930 and then effectively took power in Baghdad in December 945 under Ali, son of Buya, who declared himself *amir ul-umara* ('Great Commander'). He demanded from the Abbasid caliph al-Mustakfi (reigned 944–6) that the Buyids be allowed to rule their several territories in western Iran and Iraq as independent states. Under the nominal control of the Abbasid caliph, and with the honorific name of Imad ad-Dawlah, Ali shared power with his younger brothers Hasan and Ahmad.

The Buyid state was strongly Shiah Muslim and also had a pronounced Iranian character. Its rulers revived the Sasanian (ancient Persian) royal title of Shahanshah ('King of kings'). They were patrons of the arts, supporting both the pre-eminent Arabic poet of the day, al-Mutanabbi, and the great Persian poet Firdawsi, author of the Iranian national epic *Shahnameh* (*Book of Kings*). Their rule is known for its very fine metalwork marked with Sasanian motifs, and its pottery, some of it decorated with scenes from stories found in Firdawsi's superb epic. The Buyids encouraged

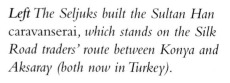

Left The Seljuks built the Sultan Han caravanserai, *which stands on the Silk Road traders' route between Konya and Aksaray (both now in Turkey).*

الخلف بين الواحد منها شابه الرزقة والاخرى يميل الى السواد
ولخا انهما انظر الى الجوق والاخرى والاخرى اسبل وكانت
اسنانه دقيقة حادة الرؤس وكان وجهه كوجه
الاسد وكان شجاعا جرئا على الحروب منها صاله نرس الله روحه

ابو لكاب الاسكندر الملك الحكيم وانه طول الدنيا

Byzantine empire at the Battle of Manzikert in 1071; the third Seljuk sultan, Malik Shah I, built on Alp Arslan's success, winning further victories over the Byzantines and defeating the Fatimids in Syria, where he established client principalities in Damascus, Aleppo and Edessa. Meanwhile, in Anatolia, his cousin, Suleyman bin Kutalmish, captured Nicaea (modern Iznik) and Nicomedia (modern Izmit) from the Byzantines in 1075 and established an independent Seljuk state in the area, called the Sultanate of Rum, with a capital at Nicaea.

The Seljuks are celebrated for restoring unity to the Islamic world under the nominal rule of a Sunni caliph. They left a great legacy to the Islamic world, building a large number of *madrasas*, or religious colleges, throughout the empire. They were also responsible for making major improvements to the Great Mosque at Isfahan, Iran, in 1086–8, adding two great brick domed chambers. Persian influence in literature, pottery and other arts continued through the Seljuks' era.

people to observe Shiah festivals and to make pilgrimages to Shiah holy places, such as Karbala and Najaf.

ERUPTION OF THE SELJUKS

In the 11th century, the Buyids were swept away by the Seljuk Turks. The Seljuks were descendants of originally Oghuz tribes from Turkestan, who had migrated southwards and settled in the Persian province of Khorasan and eventually converted to Sunni Islam. They are named after an early tribal leader, Seljuk, who led these migrations. In 1055, one of Seljuk's grandsons, Toghrul Beg, took power in Baghdad, where he was given the title 'Sultan of the East and the West' by Caliph al-Qaim (reigned 1031–75), himself no more than a figurehead.

Toghrul took control of the imperial armies in battles against the Byzantine empire and the Fatimids of Egypt. His nephew and successor as sultan, Alp Arslan ('Brave Lion'), inflicted a crushing defeat on the armies of the

Right Alaeddin Kekyubad I (reigned 1220–37) rebuilt many towns and fortresses, including the Red Tower at Alanya on the Mediterranean coast.

WARS OF THE CROSS

IN 1096-9, EUROPEAN ARMIES FIGHTING UNDER THE CROSS OF CHRIST INVADED THE MIDDLE EAST, ESTABLISHING CHRISTIAN STATES THERE. MUSLIM POWERS FOUGHT BACK IN THE 12TH CENTURY.

On 27 November 1095, at Clermont in France, Pope Urban II, leader of the Roman Catholic Church, issued a stirring call to arms to the knights (the landed warrior class) of Europe. Urban spoke out in response to a plea from Alexius Comnenus I, ruler of the Christian Byzantine empire of Constantinople, for help in fighting the Sunni Muslim Seljuk Turks. The Seljuks had established the Sultanate of Rum in central Anatolia and were threatening the Byzantine empire.

In his sermon at Clermont, Urban called on the knights of Europe to travel to the aid of their beleagured Christian brethren in Byzantine lands who were suffering terribly at the hands of 'Turks and Arabs'. According to some accounts of the speech, he also called on the knights to liberate Jerusalem, the scene of Christ's crucifixion, personifying the city and telling his listeners, 'from you, she asks for help!'

THE PEOPLE'S CRUSADE

Alexius Comnenus had envisaged an army of mercenaries; Urban directed his call at the princes, great lords and leading knights of Europe. Both were surprised: a great popular movement arose, known to historians as the People's Crusade. A 25,000-strong army, with a core of experienced soldiers supplemented by vast numbers of ill-equipped hangers-on, set out overland in April 1096 and reached Constantinople by 1 August. They crossed the Bosphorus into Anatolia but were crushed by the Seljuk Turks led by teenage Sultan Kilij Arslan I.

The few bedraggled survivors of the People's Crusade were joined by five great princely armies, led by

Above The crusader knights offered military service to Christ. They each took a vow to reach Jerusalem and pray in the Church of the Holy Sepulchre.

Count Raymond of Toulouse, Duke Robert of Normandy, Godfrey of Bouillon, Bohemond of Taranto and Hugh of Vermandois, younger brother of King Philip I of France. The united force captured Nicaea, the capital of the Sultanate of Rum in May-June 1097.

Kilij Arslan had not expected a serious assault and had departed to fight a local war; now he hurried back. But in the Battle of Dorylaeum, on 1 July 1097, he and his men were shocked by the power of the western knights' mounted charge and impressed by the strength of their chain-mail armour. They called the knights 'Franj' (for Franks, men of France, since a large part of the army was from France) and 'men of iron',

Left Godfrey of Bouillon, one of the leaders of the First Crusade, leads heavily armed and armoured crusaders in battle against Muslim warriors.

in honour of their armour. Ibn al-Qalanisi, chronicler of Damascus, wrote: 'The Franj sliced the Turkish army to pieces. They slaughtered, pillaged and seized many prisoners.'

The Christian army took Antioch in Syria from the Seljuks in June 1098, then defeated a vast relief army under Kerbogha, ruler of Mosul in the Seljuk empire. The following year, they marched on, and captured Jerusalem itself from the Shiah Muslim Fatimids of Egypt on 15–16 July 1099, slaughtering its inhabitants – Muslim and Jew alike. Arab chronicler Ibn al-Athir wrote 'The Franj spent a week slaughtering Muslims…the Jews had come together in their synagogue and the Franj roasted them alive. They also attacked the monuments of saints and the tomb of Abraham himself, may peace be upon him.' The crusaders consolidated the victory when they defeated a 50,000-strong Fatimid relief army led by the vizier (administrator) al-Afdal Shahanshah at the Battle of Ascalon on 12 August 1099.

During the crusade and in its aftermath, the westerners created four Christian territories in the Middle East: the Kingdom of Jerusalem; the County of Edessa, which was based on the ancient city of that name (now Urfa in Turkey); the Principality of Antioch; and the County of Tripoli, which was centred on that coastal city (now in Lebanon). Together these lands were known as Outremer, from the French for 'the Land overseas', so called because they lay on the far shore of the Mediterranean.

Above Capturing Antioch after a long siege in June 1098, the crusaders ran wild. Citizens fled for their lives, some leaping from the battlements in terror.

CRUSADES AND CRUSADERS

The troops who fought in 1096–9 did not call themselves crusaders: they believed they were making a journey, or *peregrinatio* (pilgrimage). Because their clothing was marked with the sign of the cross (*crux*) they became known as *crucesignati* (meaning people marked

Right In this image from an English psalm book of c.1265, Christ is depicted presiding over a map that shows Jerusalem as the centre of the world.

with the cross); they were also sometimes called the *milites Christi* (knights of Christ). The word 'crusade' was not used until the 12th–13th century.

The campaign of 1096–9 was later known as the First Crusade, because it turned out to be the first of a long series of Christian wars against Islam. Traditionally, writers numbered nine main crusades, fought in the Middle East and North Africa between 1096 and 1272, but modern historians argue that the crusades continued for many hundreds of years and were still being fought in wars against the mighty Ottoman empire in the 17th century.

MUSLIMS RESURGENT

The Artuqid Turkish ruler Ilghazi led the Muslim fightback early in the 12th century. He won a crushing victory over a Christian army in 1119 in a clash in the Principality of Antioch known to western chroniclers as the Battle of the Field of Blood. Then, in 1144, Imad ed-Din Zangi, ruler of Mosul and Aleppo, captured Edessa from its Christian rulers. A new crusade was called in 1145 and launched in 1147, but this Second Crusade was a disaster that ended in 1149 in a failed siege of Damascus.

Zengi's son Nur ed-Din took control of Damascus in 1154 and reunited Syria. A pious Sunni Muslim, Nur ad-Din was revered for just rule and commitment to his faith; he built many mosques, *caravanserais* (inns for Muslim travellers) and *madrasas*. He made a series of attempts to conquer the Shiah Muslim Fatimid regime in Egypt, which resulted, eventually, in the emergence of Salah al-Din Yusuf ibn Ayyub (later called Saladin), the nephew of Nur ad-Din's foremost general, as the vizier (administrator) of Egypt in 1169.

RIGHTEOUSNESS OF FAITH: SALADIN

SALADIN, FOUNDER OF THE SUNNI MUSLIM AYYUBID EMPIRE, PROVED A FORMIDABLE FOE TO CHRISTIAN SETTLERS IN THE HOLY LAND, FROM WHOM HE RECAPTURED JERUSALEM IN 1187.

Muslims honour Saladin for his learning, refinement and brilliance as a general – for establishing the great Ayyubid empire, uniting Muslim forces, humbling the crusader armies and recapturing the holy city of Jerusalem. But even those hounded by his armies afforded him a far-from-grudging respect, celebrating him for his military strength, proud bearing and magnanimity in victory. Indeed, in an extraordinary contradiction for 12th-century Christians, who generally believed that being a Christian lord was a key component of chivalry, they praised him as a 'chivalrous infidel'.

LEARNED AND INTELLIGENT

Salah al-Din Yusuf ibn Ayyub, more commonly known as Saladin, meaning 'Righteousness of Faith', was born in Tikrit, Iraq, to a Kurdish family. The Ayubbid dynasty he founded takes its name from that of his father, Najm ad-Din Ayyub.

He was educated in Damascus at the court of Nur ad-Din, where he studied Arabic grammar, rhetoric and Islamic theology. From early in life, Saladin was known as a refined and brilliantly intelligent man, entertaining in conversation, well versed in the traditions of Arab tribes, an expert in the genealogies of the best Arab horses, and a peerless polo player.

He also had a brilliant military upbringing, serving alongside his uncle Shirkuh, Nur ad-Din's leading general, with whom he three times invaded Egypt in the 1160s. On the third campaign in Egypt, Saladin helped his uncle oust the Fatimid vizier Shawar, establishing Shirkuh as vizier and then succeeding him in the position on his death just three months later.

RISE TO POWER

As vizier of Egypt, Saladin was nominally subject to Nur ad-Din, but his scarcely concealed desire was to take power himself and unite Syria and Egypt in a new empire,

Above Saladin's fame in Christendom meant that he was the subject of European works of art, such as this 16th-century Italian portrait.

and he became increasingly estranged from his overlord. Nur ad-Din and Saladin were both Sunni Muslims and one initial point of his conflict was Saladin's refusal to oust the Shiah Fatimid caliph in Cairo, al-Adid. Saladin waited until al-Adid died in September 1171, then ended the Fatimid caliphate and declared the authority of al-Mustadi, the Sunni Abbasid caliph in Baghdad.

Below Saladin and Richard 'Coeur de Lion' were exemplars of chivalry. This (imagined) jousting clash between them is from the English Luttrell Psalter.

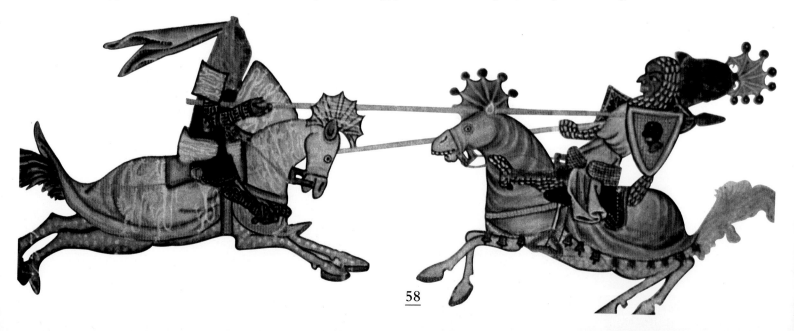

Matters came to a head on Nur ad-Din's death, from fever, in 1174. Saladin marched to Damascus, where he was welcomed by the people. He bolstered his position by marrying Nur ad-Din's widow and publicly setting himself up as leader of a *jihad*, or a 'just war', against the Christian kingdoms of the Middle East. He established his authority in Syria, northern Iraq, the Hejaz and Yemen and led several campaigns against the Christians, culminating in the Battle of the Horns of Hattin in 1187. Here, he captured the most sacred relic of the Christians – reputedly a piece of the cross on which Jesus Christ was crucified – and destroyed the military strength of the kingdom of Jerusalem.

ENCOUNTERS WITH COEUR DE LION

After capturing Jerusalem in 1187, Saladin encountered the Christian armies of the Third Crusade (1189–92) led by Richard I *Coeur de Lion* ('the Lion-hearted') of England and King Philip II of France. In Richard, Saladin met his match, and the encounter of these two great generals was widely celebrated in European chivalric literature, ensuring Saladin undying fame in the West as well as the East.

Although he twice marched towards Jerusalem, Richard did not attempt to retake it, and the Third Crusade ended in a negotiated settlement at the treaty of Jaffa, under which the Christians were guaranteed access to Jerusalem as pilgrims and could keep certain chiefly coastal territories, including the ports of Acre and Jaffa.

Saladin died at Damascus on 4 March 1193, shortly after the end of the crusade, and was buried in a mausoleum beside the Umayyad Mosque in Damascus. A member of Saladin's entourage, Baha ud-Din ibn Shaddad, wrote a biography, in which he praised his master's

character and his unswerving commitment to *jihad*. According to Baha ud-Din, Saladin did not spend a single coin on anything other than *jihad* and pious work and was a fascinating and learned man, who would not hear ill spoken of other Muslims and was always caring for the elderly and for orphans.

Above Saladin lost twice to Richard 'the Lion-hearted' in 1191, at Acre and Arsuf, and at Jaffa in September 1192 agreed a peace treaty.

Below Saladin's tomb in Damascus. Kaiser Wilhelm II of Germany donated a marble sarcophagus, but Saladin's body lies in the wooden one at the rear.

THE BATTLE OF BAGHDAD

THE NOMINAL RULE OF THE ABBASID CALIPHATE IN BAGHDAD ENDED IN 1258, WHEN AN INVADING MONGOL ARMY DESTROYED THE CITY, BUT THE ABBASIDS SURVIVED IN EGYPT UNTIL THE 16TH CENTURY.

The Battle of Baghdad, which took place in January and February 1258 between the city's defenders and a vast besieging Mongol army, was a devastating event for the Muslims of the Middle East. The attack culminated in a week-long orgy of pillaging and looting, from which the beautiful city of Baghdad took centuries to recover. The Mongol army moved on, and with the support of local Christian powers, conquered Aleppo and Damascus in 1260. In just two years, the two great centres of Islamic power in the Middle East, Baghdad and Damascus, were lost. The principal surviving centre of Muslim rule in the East was Mamluk Egypt.

BACKGROUND TO THE CONFLICT

By the mid-13th century, the Abbasid caliphate in Baghdad had regained a measure of power, although the caliphs were still essentially dependent for their position on the Turkish and Mamluk military power. In 1258,

Above When the Mongols took Baghdad, the last Abbasid caliph, al-Mustasim, was captured and forced to watch the destruction of his city.

Below A 14th-century manuscript painting shows the Mongol army making preparations prior to attacking Baghdad.

the caliph was al-Mustasim Billah (reigned 1242–58). His opponent, Hulagu Khan, who was a grandson of Genghis Khan, had been despatched by his brother Mongke, the Great Kahn, to lead the military destruction of Islamic states in Iran, Iraq and Syria.

Commanded by Hulagu and Chinese general Guo Kan, a vast Mongol army, which reputedly contained a tenth of the fighting force of the entire Mongol empire, approached Baghdad in November 1257 and initially offered a peaceful takeover. Although he had made no preparations for the assault, al-Mustasim was defiant. Evidently unable to appreciate the gravity of the situation, or else deliberately deluding himself, he had reputedly accepted the advice of his vizier that the Mongols would be easily driven away by the simple tactic of ordering the women of Baghdad to throw stones at them.

THE FALL OF BAGHDAD

The Mongol army laid siege to the city on 29 January, and on 10 February, al-Mustasim surrendered. The Mongols swept into the city, pillaging, raping and looting, and hundreds of thousands of people were killed as they tried to flee.

Mosques, libraries, hospitals and palaces were burned down. The invaders did not spare even the Grand Library, repository of much of the wisdom of the ancient world: one account reports that the river Tigris was turned black with the ink from the manuscripts hurled into its waters.

The Mongol army moved on from Baghdad to attack and capture Damascus from its last Ayyubid ruler, An-Nasir Yusuf, in alliance with Christian armies from the Principality of Antioch and Cilician Armenia.

THE RISE OF THE MAMLUKS IN EGYPT

Following Saladin's death in 1193, the Ayyubid empire he had created survived for around 50 years, with Ayyubid lords in power in Syria and Egypt. In 1250, however, the Ayyubid sultan of Egypt, Turanshah, was murdered. His Mamluk slave general, Izz al-Din Aybak, took power and founded the Mamluk sultanate, which ruled Egypt (and later Syria) until 1517.

The Mamluk army won a series of astounding victories, defeating the previously invincible Mongols at the Battle of Ain Jalut in 1260 and afterwards driving the Christians from the Holy Land. To

Above Mamluk general Baybar was ruthless in conflict: it is said he beheaded Christian knights who had surrendered in the belief that they would be spared.

legitimate their rule, Mamluk sultans re-established the Abbasid caliphate, now in Cairo rather than Baghdad. The first caliph under this dispensation was al-Mustansir (reigned 1226–42). With strictly nominal authority, Abbasid caliphs succeeded one another in Cairo until 1517, when, after Ottoman sultan Selim I defeated the Mamluks, the final Abbasid caliph al-Mutawakkil III was taken to Constantinople. On al-Mutawakkil's death, by prior agreement, the title of caliph passed to Selim I.

END OF OUTREMER

After the loss of Jerusalem to Saladin in 1187, the capital of the Christian kingdom of Jerusalem was moved to Acre. In the late 13th century, the crusader states lost a series of their territorial possessions – including Arsuf, Caesarea, Antioch and Tripoli – to the armies of the Egyptian Mamluk sultans. The Christians made a last stand in Acre in 1291, but, despite heroic defensive efforts by the military orders of the Knights Templar and Knights Hospitaller, the city was captured by the Mamluk sultan Khalil on 18 May 1291. Within a few weeks, the final remaining crusader towns of Beirut, Haifa, Tyre and Tortosa were surrendered to the Mamluks. The Christian kingdoms of Outremer were at an end.

Left Astride the city's crumbling walls, French knight Guillaume de Clermont leads the final stand of the kingdom of Jerusalem as Acre falls to the Mamluks.

LIGHT IN THE DARKNESS

THE SCHOLARS OF ISLAMIC BAGHDAD AND CAIRO KEPT THE FLAME
OF SCHOLARSHIP ALIGHT AT A TIME KNOWN AS THE 'CHRISTIAN DARK
AGES', WHEN LEARNING WAS NOT GREATLY VALUED IN EUROPE.

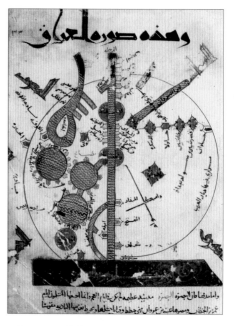

Above Baghdad, great centre of learning, is marked on this page from the 11th-century Book of Routes and Provinces *by Abu Ishaq Ibrahim al-Istakhri.*

When European cultural life enjoyed a Renaissance, or 'rebirth', in the 14th century, much of its knowledge of classical Greek, Roman and other ancient learning came from translations into Latin of Islamic authors who had written in Arabic at the Abbasid House of Wisdom in Baghdad and at other Islamic establishments of learning.

THE TRANSMISSION OF KNOWLEDGE

The principal works of Islamic mathematician Muhammad ibn Musa al-Khwarizmi (*c.*780–*c.*850) were translated into Latin, and introduced Europe to the concept of what came to be known as the Arabic numerals, the concept of zero and the positional value system. Another highly influential mathematical work was the *Book of Measuring Plane and Spherical Figures*, which was translated into Latin by the Lombardian scholar Gerard of Cremona (*c.*1114–87). Gerard also translated into Latin

Ibn Sina's *Canon of Medicine* and the key writings of Aristotle from Arabic translations made in the 9th century by gifted Mesopotamian linguist Thabit ibn Qurra (known in Latin as Thebit), who worked at the House of Wisdom. The *Canon* of Ibn Sina became a key medical textbook in western universities and was still in use in some places in the mid-17th century.

The translator Hunain ibn Ishaq's work on ophthalmology was likewise translated into Latin and became a key reference book in universities both in Europe and in the East for many hundreds of years. Arab philospher al-Farabi (*c.*878–*c.*950) wrote a book called *The Catalogue of Sciences*, in which he noted the following key areas of study, listed in order of importance: languages, logic, mathematics, physics, metaphysics, politics, law and theology. Later translated into Latin, the work became a major influence on the curricula of study that was followed in many early European universities.

AL-ANDALUS

Classical philosophy and learning was also preserved and passed to Western European scholars through the work of Islamic thinkers and authors in al-Andalus, the Muslim territories of the Iberian Peninsula. A key figure was Abu'l-Walid Muhammad ibn Ahmad ibn Rushd (1126–98), known in the West as Averroes. Another great Muslim polymath, he wrote on philosophy, theology, law, medicine, astrology, geography and physics. Among his works were a medical encyclopedia and commentaries on the *Canon* of Ibn Sina and the works of Aristotle and Plato, for which his sources were the Arabic translations made in the 10th century in Iraq.

SCHOLARLY PRACTICES

A number of key scholarly methods were pioneered at the House of Wisdom, many of which are still in

Left East meets West in this painting by Julius Köckert as Harun al-Rashid receives envoys from Charlemagne, King of the Franks, in Baghdad.

Above *One of the great Islamic scholars of Spain, Averroes wrote commentaries on the works of Aristotle and Plato for Almohad caliph Abu Yaqub Yusuf.*

use today, for example a library catalogue system in which works are categorized by genre or other characteristics. Scholars at the House of Wisdom were also the first to collate various manuscripts of a work in order to make a definitive edition, to add annotations to the margins of works, to write glossaries and to draw up dictionaries of key technical words.

REASON AND REVELATION

The Islamic scholars who saved so much classical learning for future generations had a deep intellectual curiosity and profound commitment to the study of philosophy, mathematics and logic, medicine, mechanics and physics.

At first sight, it might seem curious that adherents of a faith founded on Allah's revelation of truth to the Prophet Muhammad should be interested in the

Right *Ancient Greek philosopher Aristotle was honoured by many Islamic thinkers. He wrote on theatre and politics, on logic, ethics and physics.*

reasonings of pagan thinkers from the ancient world. But Islam had a strong commitment to learning from the beginning. Muslims are enjoined to seek knowledge by the Prophet himself: according to hadith literature, Muhammad said 'Seeking knowledge is obligatory for every Muslim' and 'go after learning, even to China'.

Muslim chronicles recount how philosopher Aristotle (384–22BCE) appeared to the Abbasid caliph al-Mamun, founder of the House of Wisdom, in a dream. The Aristotle of the dream was a figure of profound beauty, and when al-Mamun asked him the cause of his beauty, Aristotle replied that it derived from 'the beauty of the laws of reason'. Aristotle also assured al-Mamun that there was no clash between the human reason he exercised and praised and the revelation of God's law to the Prophet Muhammad.

AL-ANDALUS

ISLAMIC RULERS GOVERNED PART OF THE IBERIAN PENINSULA FOR ALMOST 800 YEARS. MUSLIM LANDS, WHICH INCLUDED THE CITIES OF CÓRDOBA, SEVILLE AND GRANADA, WERE KNOWN AS AL-ANDALUS.

The Arab–Berber invasion of the Iberian Peninsula, begun in April 711, was one more in a series of stunning military successes for the armies of Islam. Under first Tariq ibn Ziyad and then Musa bin Nusair, the Islamic troops captured almost the entire peninsula in only five years. The land was initially a province of the Umayyad caliphate under overall rule of Caliph al-Walid I (reigned 705–15) in Damascus. From 717, this province made its capital at Córdoba.

In these early years, the Christian Visigoths, previous rulers of much of the Iberian Peninsula, were driven to the far north, but there they maintained a foothold that proved to be the base for a centuries-long fight back, known to Christian historians as the *Reconquista* ('Reconquest').

EMIRATE OF CÓRDOBA

In Iraq, the Hashimiyyah revolt led to the establishment of the Abassid caliphate by Abu al-Abbas in 750, and Abd al-Rahman, sole surviving member of the Umayyad royal family, fled to what is now southern Spain. In 756, he defeated the ruler of Al-Andalus, Yusuf al-Fihri, in battle, and set himself up as Amir of Córdoba, an independent Umayyad ruler in opposition to the Abbasids in Baghdad.

Abd al-Rahman ruled in Córdoba until *c.*788. He put down a number of revolts, including a major uprising backed by Abbasid caliph al-Mansur (reigned 754–75) and led by al-Ala ibn Mugith, who was the governor of the province of Ifriqiya (Africa). Besieged in Carmona, Abd al-Rahman led a daring breakout, defeating the Abbasid troops. He then sent the heads of al-Ala and his generals, pickled in salt, in a bag all the way to Makkah, where al-Mansur was making the *Hajj*.

Left The Reconquista *was gathering pace by the 9th century. However, the heroic victory of Christian King Ramiro at the Battle of Clavijo (844), shown here, is in fact legendary.*

Above The Arab–Berber army under Tariq ibn Ziyad captures Córdoba in 711. The city would remain in Muslim hands until 1236.

CALIPHATE OF CÓRDOBA

Abd al-Rahman III (reigned 912–61) was the most powerful of the Umayyad rulers in Spain. In 929, he defied the Abassids and the rising power of the Fatimids in Egypt by declaring himself Caliph of Córdoba, claiming authority over the entire Islamic world. He won several victories against the Christian kings of northern Spain and was hailed as *al-Nasir* ('Defender of the Faith').

During the reign of Abd al-Rahman III and his son al-Hakam II, Al-Andalus was at the height of its glory, but decline set in within 50 years of his death in 961. The caliphate did not recover from civil war among rival claimants to power in 1010, although it limped on until 1031, when it was broken up into smaller *taifa* ('successor') kingdoms.

ALMORAVIDS AND ALMOHADS

These *taifa* states proved vulnerable to the advance of the Christian kingdoms of northern Iberia and

then were swept away by the Almoravids, a Berber power from North Africa. The Almoravid ruler Yusuf ibn Tashfin declared himself as *Amir al-Muslimin* ('Commander of the Muslims') in opposition to the caliph in Baghdad, who was revered as *Amir al-Mumineen* ('Commander of the Faithful').

Power switched hands again in the second half of the 12th century, when Abu Ya'qub Yusuf, leader of another Berber confederation, called the Almohads, took control of Muslim Iberia and established his capital at Seville. Abu Ya'qub Yusuf was known as al-Mansur ('the Victorious') following his great victory over King Alfonso VIII of Castile in the Battle of Alarcos on 19 July 1195. However, his successor, Muhammad III al-Nasir, suffered a devastating defeat in the Battle of Las Navas de Tolosa on 16 July 1212 at the hands of a Christian army. Following this defeat, the power of the Almohads unravelled swiftly, and King Ferdinand III of

Above Islamic rule in Spain ends as Sultan Boabdil surrenders Granada to crusaders led by Ferdinand and Isabella.

Below Ferdinand and Isabella are depicted leading their troops into Granada in 1492 in a wooden panel from an altarpiece of c.1522.

Castile recaptured the great Islamic cities of Córdoba in 1236 and of Seville in 1248.

Thereafter, the sole surviving Islamic territory in Iberia was the Muslim kingdom of Granada in the far south, which was ruled from 1232 by the Nasrid dynasty, or Banu Nazari, as a client state of the local Christian kingdoms.

LAST STAND IN GRANADA

The days of Islamic rule in al-Andalus were numbered, yet remarkably – principally because of infighting among the Christian kingdoms – the end did not come until 1492. Besieged in Granada by a Christian army that was equipped with the latest weaponry and bolstered by crusading troops from many parts of Europe, Nasrid sultan Boabdil surrendered. After making a triumphant entry into Granada, the fervently Catholic King Ferdinand and Queen Isabella set about rebuilding the main mosque as a church.

THE ISLAMIC RENAISSANCE IN SPAIN

THE YEARS OF ISLAMIC RULE IN SPAIN, NOTABLY UNDER THE CALIPHATE OF CÓRDOBA (929–1031), WERE A GLORIOUS AGE OF LEARNING, ARTISTIC ACHIEVEMENT AND RELIGIOUS TOLERATION.

Abd al-Rahman III, the man who proclaimed himself caliph in Córdoba in 929, was a great patron of architecture and reputedly spent one-third of the income from his vast territories on building works. Beginning in 936–40, he built the palace-city of Madinat al-Zahra outside Córdoba. Although little remains of the city today – it was sacked in 1010 during the civil war that brought the caliphate to its knees – it was once vast and magnificent, described in accounts by contemporary travellers as a series of palaces filled with extraordinary treasures.

GLORIES OF CÓRDOBA
Caliph Abd al-Rahman III greatly developed Córdoba itself. Scholars estimate that in the 10th century, the city had a population of up to 500,000 people. He built a new minaret for the superb mosque in Córdoba, begun in 784 by dynastic founder Abd al-Rahman I. This magnificent sacred building, which was originally called the Aljama Mosque in honour of Abd al-Rahman I's wife but is now known as the Mezquita of Córdoba, was built on the site of a 6th-century Christian church. The mosque was further extended by Abd al-Rahman III's son, al-Hakam II, and work on it continued until 987. After Córdoba was captured by King Ferdinand III of Castile in 1236, the building was reconsecrated as a church, and today it is a Christian cathedral, although its celebrated arches, beautiful blue-tiled dome and magnificent *mihrab* can still be seen.

The second caliph in Córdoba, al-Hakam II, made peace with the northern Christian kingdoms

Above Abd al-Rahman III: according to legend, he named his palace city outside Córdoba after his foremost concubine and raised her statue over the main gateway.

and concentrated his efforts and wealth on the improvement of the caliphate's infrastructure and the advancement of learning. Under his rule, irrigation works advanced agriculture, while in cities, the building of markets and widening of streets promoted commerce.

In Córdoba, al-Hakam II created a vast library containing 400,000 books and established a committee of learned men, including both Arab Muslims and Mozarab Christians, to translate works from Latin and Greek into Arabic. (Mozarab Christians were the descendants of Iberian Christians who had lived on under Muslim rule and, while keeping to their own faith, had adopted Arabic customs and language.)

Left The illuminated Mezquita, begun in 784 by Abd al-Rahman I, looks down on the Guadalquivir, the longest river in Andalucía, which connects Córdoba to the Gulf of Cadiz.

Left The beautiful octagonal dome in the Mezquita rises above the mihrab and maqsura enclosure and was built by al-Hakam II.

conquered the city. However, because it was so well established as an international centre of learning under Islam, it remained a meeting place for scholars, where both Arabs and Jews were welcome and Christian scholars, such as Gerard of Cremona (*c.*1114–87), could come to meet them.

RELIGIOUS TOLERATION

This great cultural flowering of Al-Andalus was made possible – as had been the golden age under the Abbasid caliphs in Baghdad – by a remarkable degree of religious toleration. Despite the fact that for almost the entire history of Al-Andalus, the territory's Islamic rulers were engaged in a stop-start war against Christians seeking to win control of the Iberian Peninsula, within Al-Andalus itself, Muslims, Jews and Mozarab Christians were able to live in peace, and together played a major role in the cultural flowering of Islamic Spain.

CENTRES OF LEARNING

The great cities of Al-Andalus, such as Toledo and Córdoba, were the intellectual capitals of Western Europe. Students came from as far away as England and northern France to learn from the Arab, Jewish and Christian scholars who gathered there.

The great Jewish poet, physician, astrologer and scholar, Abraham ben Meir ibn Ezra (1093–1167), was born in Tudela under Muslim rule and lived for many years in Córdoba. Jewish philosopher and physician Moshe ben Maimon, better known by his Greek name Moses Maimonides and generally recognized as the greatest Jewish

philosopher of the Middle Ages, was also a product of this culture, and was born in Córdoba in 1135.

Córdoba was celebrated for its copyists, producers of religious manuscripts, and artisans, who made leatherwork, jewellery, brocades and woven silks that were among the best in the world and were traded both in Western Europe and across the markets of the East.

Toledo was a great centre for scholars, home both to a large community of Mozarab Christians and a sizeable Jewish colony. Conquered for Islam by Tariq ibn Ziyad in 711, it was part of Al-Andalus until 1085, when Christian King Alfonso VI of Leon

Right Jewish philosopher Moses Maimonides rose to prominence in Córdoba, then lived in Morocco and in Egypt, where he was doctor to Saladin.

ISLAM IN ASIA

AFTER MUSLIM AFGHANS ESTABLISHED THE DELHI SULTANATE IN THE LATE 1100S, ISLAM BECAME A MAJOR FORCE BOTH IN THE INDIAN SUBCONTINENT AND BEYOND IN MALAYA, SUMATRA AND JAVA.

In 711, Arab troops under Syrian general Muhammad ibn-Qasim conquered Sindh (in the south-east of modern Pakistan), and many locals converted to Islam. However, there were no further invasions until Muslim Afghan ruler Mahmud of Ghazni launched a series of raids from eastern Afghanistan in the 11th century. Mahmud achieved control over much of north-west India and what is now Pakistan, but he came principally to loot the wealth of temples, and his rule was only periodically enforced.

The first permanent Muslim presence in India was achieved by the troops of another Afghan ruler, Muhammad of Ghor, when they captured Delhi in 1193. Muhammad's general, Qutb-ud-din Aybak, declared himself Sultan of Delhi (reigned 1206–10) and founded the Mamluk dynasty, first of the Delhi sultanate. By c.1235, the Mamluks had taken control of the whole of northern India.

TUGHLUQ POWER

The Delhi sultanate ruled India until 1526. In the 14th century, its sultans achieved power over almost the entire subcontinent under the Tughluq dynasty. Only the native Pandava kings (in the far south) and Rajputs (in the north-west) held them at bay.

However the sultanate's power was smashed in a devastating raid on Delhi unleashed in 1398 by

Right The tomb of the second ruler of the Mughal dynasty, Humayan, in Delhi has Persian-style gardens and was built in 1562–70.

Timur (or Tamerlane), Mongol ruler of Samarkand. Thereafter, the sultanate could not recover its former status, although it survived until 1526, when Ibrahim Lodhi was defeated in battle by Afghan ruler Babur at Panipat, north of Delhi. Babur went on to conquer large parts of India and to found the Mughal dynasty, which created a vast Islamic empire in the region.

MUGHAL GLORIES

The Mughal state founded by Babur suffered early setbacks but was doubled in size and established as an empire by Akbar the Great in 1556–1605. By 1600, his empire covered most of north India as far south as the river Narmada. The empire continued to grow under his sons Jahangir and Shah Jahan, and achieved its greatest extent, covering the entire Indian subcontinent save the southern tip, in c.1700 under Aurangzeb.

Above This scene from the superb Hamzanama, *created at the court of Akbar the Great in c.1562–77, shows an escape from prison.*

Akbar the Great presided over a magnificent court with a vibrant cultural life. He created a vast library, with books in English, Greek, Persian and Hindi as well as Arabic and including Hindu scriptures and the Bible. He also oversaw the creation of an illustrated manuscript of the *Hamzanama*, an originally Persian romance, telling the adventures of a fictional uncle of

dynasty (618-907). China's first mosque was built in Guangzhou at this time. A modest number of Arab and Persian merchants settled in China and became dominant in the import/export trade. Then, under the Mongol Yuan dynasty (1274–1368), Muslims settled in China in large numbers, where they served as administrators for the Mongol rulers.

Islam was also a major force elsewhere in Asia. The Sultanate of Malacca in southern Malaysia was an important Islamic regional power at its height in the 15th century, while the Sultanate of Demak on the north coast of Java in Indonesia was founded in the late 15th century. The Masjid Agung Demak, or Great Demak Mosque, in Demak, on Java, was built at this time. The Sultanate of Aceh was another important Islamic regional power, with its base in Sumatra, Indonesia, in the 16th and 17th centuries. Its capital was Kutaraja (modern Banda Aceh).

the Prophet Muhammad, Amir Hamza. With 1,400 canvas miniature illustrations, this manuscript is one of the masterpieces of Islamic art.

Akbar rebuilt the celebrated red fort of Agra and constructed nearby the city of Fatehpur Sikri as his capital. His grandson, Shah Jahan, built the most celebrated of all Mughal monuments, the Taj Mahal in Agra (1632–54), to house the tomb of his favoured wife, Mumtaz Mahal. He also built the magnificent Jama Masjid, one of India's most famous mosques, in Delhi in 1656.

Ultimately, the Mughal empire declined in the face of a rival Hindu confederation, the Maratha empire, and the growing power of the British East India Company in the region. Nevertheless, it survived in various forms until 1857, when the last emperor, Bahadur Shah II (reigned 1838–57), was exiled to Rangoon in Burma by the British.

BEYOND INDIA

Islam was introduced to China in 651, within 20 years of the death of the Prophet Muhammad, when the latter's maternal uncle Saad ibn Abi Waqqas was sent as an envoy to Gaozong, an emperor of the Tang

Right The Kampung Kling Mosque in Malacca, Malaysia, was built in 1748, using the traditional square design of the earliest mosques.

BEYOND THE SAHARA

ISLAM WAS ESTABLISHED IN NORTHERN AFRICA IN THE EARLY DAYS OF
THE FAITH, AND SPREAD SOUTHWARD ALONG TRADE ROUTES. MAJOR
AFRICAN ISLAMIC EMPIRES INCLUDED THE MALI AND SONGHAI.

Arab Muslims had invaded Egypt in 639 during the reign of Caliph Umar (634–44), capturing Alexandria in 643 and establishing Sunni Islam there. The faith had spread along the north of the continent as far as Morocco by 711, when general Tariq ibn Ziyad carried it across the Straits of Gibraltar into the Iberian Peninsula. Right from these early days, Arab trade caravans bore the Islamic faith along with their goods as they made their way across the Sahara into sub-Saharan Africa. At around the same time, Arab merchants sailed down Africa's east coast and established Islamic trading ports there.

GHANA EMPIRE

In western Sudan, between the upper Senegal and Niger rivers, an empire called the Ghana, or Wagadou ('Land of Herding'), grew very rich on trade in gold, ivory and slaves from the 8th century onward. The empire was ruled by a Muslim elite and was at its height in c.1050. It is said to have comprised two linked cities, one inhabited by Muslims, containing at least 12 mosques and the royal palace, and a second around 10km (6 miles) away for the pagan natives.

The capital was sacked by the Muslim Almoravids of Morocco in 1076. Then, in the 13th century, the lands of the Ghana empire were

Above The 14th-century Djinguereber Mosque in Timbuktu, Mali, is made entirely from mud, straw and wood. It has space for 2,000 people to pray.

Below The Great Mosque of Djenné in Mali is the world's largest mud-brick building. The mosque was built in 1907 on foundations dating from the 1200s.

subsumed by a new power, the kingdom of Mali, established by a Muslim ruler named Sundiata Keita in *c*.1240.

MALI EMPIRE

Beginning from a small state on the upper Niger River, Sundiata Keita conquered many neighbouring kingdoms and created a sizeable state that acquired enormous wealth from controlling trade throughout West Africa and even beyond, to Asia and Europe.

Sundiata Keita's great-nephew Mansu Musa (reigned 1312–37) conquered the cities of Timbuktu and Gao and established Mali as a great empire. A celebrated account survives of the *Hajj* pilgrimage to Makkah that Mansu Musa made in 1324: when passing through Cairo he gave so many gifts of gold that it created inflation across Egypt.

Mansu Musa brought the Arabian architect and poet Abu Es Haq Es Saheli back from Makkah and, under his influence, built religious schools and a university in Timbuktu. In 1327, Es Saheli built the Djinguereber Mosque in Timbuktu. Along with the mosques of Sankoré and Sidi Yahya, it formed part of the university, which itself played a major role in the spread of Islam in Africa.

SONGHAI EMPIRE

The Mali empire thrived until the mid-15th century, when it was eclipsed by another West African Muslim state, the kingdom of the Songhai. Under Ali the Great (reigned 1465–92) and Askia Muhammad I (reigned 1492–1528), the Songhai created a trading empire to rival that of the Mali. Its leaders were just as devout as their predecessors and fostered the growth of learning in Timbuktu. Under Askia Muhammad's rule, scholars made translations of ancient Greek philosophers Plato

Above The Sankoré Mosque in Timbuktu was built in the 15th century. Its courtyard is said to have been built to match the dimensions of the Kaabah.

and Aristotle, Abd al-Rahman al-Sadi compiled the great African history *Tarikh al-Sudan* ('Chronicles of Africa') and the great legal scholar Ahmed Baba was at work.

The Songhai empire survived until 1591, when it was crushed by a Moroccan invasion, and afterward, minor kingdoms attempted without success to fill the gap left by the Mali and Songhai.

In West-central Africa, the Muslim Kanem–Borno empire to the north and west of Lake Chad was at its height in the 16th century. Under Mai Idris Alooma (reigned 1571–1603), the imperial army used firearms purchased from the Ottoman Turks to take control of trade with Egypt and Libya. The empire faded after *c*.1650, but survived in name until 1846, when it was eclipsed by another regional power, the Adai empire.

EAST AFRICAN CITY-STATES

In East Africa, Muslim Arab traders settled along the coast from *c*.900 and created city-states such as Mogadishu (today the capital of Somalia), Mombasa and Malindi

(both now in Kenya), and Kilwa Kisiwani (an island port off the coast of modern Tanzania). Islam spread inland from these port cities, and in East Africa became better established among the people than in West Africa, where the faith remained largely the preserve of the governing elite for many years.

Above The atmospheric prayer hall of the Great Mosque on the island of Kilwa Kisiwani is still standing. The mosque was founded in the 900s and rebuilt in the 11th and 12th centuries.

LAND OF THE SHAHS

FROM 1502 UNTIL 1722, THE SHIAH MUSLIM SAFAVIDS RULED A
GREAT ISLAMIC EMPIRE IN PERSIA. WITH ITS MAGNIFICENT CAPITAL AT
ISFAHAN, IT WAS AT ITS HEIGHT UNDER SHAH ABBAS I IN THE 1620S.

The rise of the Safavids was a major development in the history of Islam: theirs was the first large and enduring Shiah Muslim state since the Fatimids. They established the Shiah branch of the faith as the dominant form of Islam in the Caucasus and much of western Asia, especially Iran.

The Safavids were descended from Turkish adherents of the mystical branch of Sunni Islam named Sufism who had converted to Shiah Islam in the 15th century. They came to believe that they were called to spread Shiah Islam through military conquest.

THE 'HIDDEN IMAM'

At the start of the 16th century, a young Safavid leader, Ismail, claimed to be a representative of the 'Hidden Imam', the 12th Shiah imam Muhammad al-Mahdi. According to Shiah tradition, after the 11th Shiah imam, Hassan al-Askari, was killed in 874, his successor was hidden by Allah through a process called *ghaybah* (occultation) in order to

Below The beautiful Imam Mosque in Isfahan, central Iran, was built by Abbas I in 1611–29. The minarets flanking the main gateway are 42m (137ft) high.

Above The greatest of Safavid rulers, Abbas I, restored the dynasty's power, winning a string of military victories.

save his life. Shiah Muslims claim that he remains miraculously alive and will one day return to guide the faithful. In this guise, Ismail gained a

ISFAHAN

In central Iran, Abbas I built a new capital alongside the ancient city of the Sasanians. At its peak, Isfahan was one of the wonders of the world: it had no fewer than 163 mosques, more than 250 public baths and around 1,800 shops. The city was also rich in beautiful parks, large squares, libraries and religious schools. The mosques included the stunning Shah Mosque, begun in 1611, with its elegant calligraphic inscriptions and mosaic tiling; it is often described as one of the world's greatest examples of mosque architecture.

devoted following, despite the fact that he was only 12 years old, and led troops to capture the kingdom of Shirvan (now part of Azerbaijan) and the city of Tabriz. He declared himself Shah of Azerbaijan, and proclaimed the Shiah faith to be the official religion in his lands.

Ismail then announced that he was the Hidden Imam himself, returned to rule and to lead the faithful. Within ten years, Ismail had taken control of all of Iran, and captured Baghdad and Mosul in Iraq. In the north-east, he defeated and drove back the Uzbeks.

OTTOMANS HIT BACK

The Safavids now posed a threat to the might of the Ottoman empire: Ismail's Shiah missionaries converted many Turkmen tribes in Ottoman territories in Anatolia and Iraq. Ottoman sultan Selim I marched into Iran and defeated Ismail in the Battle of Chaldiran in 1514. Though wounded and nearly captured, Ismail survived, but his position was seriously weakened, for he lost his aura of invincibility.

The Safavid empire was crucially undermined during the reigns of the next three shahs, Tahmasp I

Above In the elegant Ali Ghapu palace on Nagsh-i Jahan Square, Isfahan, Abbas I received ambassadors and dignitaries from around the world.

(1524–76), Ismail II (1576–77) and Muhammad Khudabanda (1578–88), which saw civil war and internal power struggles as well as repeated attacks by the Ottomans and the Uzbeks, but the dynasty rose to the height of its power and glory under Abbas I (1587–1629).

CONQUESTS OF ABBAS I

The Safavids had lost Baghdad and much of Iraq to the Ottomans, and Abbas recognized that his army needed updating. He negotiated a peace treaty with the Ottomans, and, with the help of two Englishmen, Anthony and Robert Shirley, set about reorganizing the military on the European model of a standing army fully equipped with artillery and muskets.

The new force recaptured Herat and Mashhad from the Uzbeks, and then Baghdad, the eastern part of Iraq and the provinces in the Caucasus from the Ottomans. He regained control of the port of Hormuz on the Persian Gulf from

Above A superb edition of Iran's national epic, the 11th-century Shahnahmeh *by Firdawsi, was made for Shah Tahmasp I.*

the English and developed lucrative trading links with the Dutch and English East India companies.

Following the death of Abbas I in 1629, the Safavid empire endured for around 100 years, but this was generally a period of slow decline, enlivened only by the reign of Abbas II (1642–66). The Safavid dynasty ended in 1760, when Karim Khan Zand founded the Zand dynasty.

RISE OF THE OTTOMANS

FROM MODEST BEGINNINGS IN THE 14TH CENTURY, TURKISH TRIBES IN ANATOLIA CREATED THE GREATEST ISLAMIC EMPIRE IN HISTORY, THE OTTOMAN EMPIRE, WHICH LASTED FOR MORE THAN 600 YEARS.

The Ottoman dynastic founder, Osman, was a descendant of the nomadic Kayi tribe, originally from Turkestan in central Asia, who settled in Anatolia in the 12th century and established a base in Söğüt, north-western Anatolia (now in Turkey) in the late 13th century. According to one legend, Osman's father, Ertugrul, was leading a force of around 400 horsemen across the region when he chanced upon a battle: he joined in support of the losing side and turned the conflict in their favour, and as a reward the Seljuk sultan he had helped gave him land on which to settle.

Osman (reigned 1258–1324) expanded the territory, and under his son Orhan (reigned 1324–60), the Ottomans became a major regional power. Among other cities, Orhan captured Bursa (in 1326), which he made into a great centre for Islam. He also helped John Kantakouzenos take the Byzantine imperial throne from his rival John V Palaeologus and was rewarded with the hand of the emperor's daughter, Theodora, in marriage and the right to raid with impunity in Thrace (a historical region of south-eastern Europe).

THE FIRST SULTAN

Orhan's son Murad I (reigned 1359–89) expanded Ottoman power in Thrace. He was the first Ottoman ruler to adopt the title sultan, in 1383. He founded a number of enduring Ottoman institutions, including the elite military corps of the Janissaries, and the offices of *beylerbeyi* (military commander-in-chief) and grand vizier (principal government minister).

Within the rapidly expanding empire, the Ottomans allowed local rulers to remain in nominal control so long as they paid annual tribute and provided troops for the imperial army. Many Christian rulers in south-east Europe, and even the Byzantine emperor John V, became client rulers under Ottoman overlordship.

Above Osman's name means 'breaker of bones' and Ottoman writers saw in this a prophecy of the military strength of the empire he founded.

THE THUNDERBOLT

Murad's son Bayezid I (reigned 1389–1402) was known as *Yildirim* ('Thunderbolt') because of the speed of his military campaigns. He imposed Ottoman authority in Anatolia, then occupied Bulgaria, and, though the Europeans launched a crusade against him, he defeated them in the Battle of Nicopolis in 1396. Bayezid maintained a siege of Constantinople for no less than seven years (1391–98), but he met his match in the Mongol leader Timur (or Tamerlane), who invaded Anatolia and defeated the Ottomans at the Battle of Ankara in 1402. Bayezid died in captivity the following year.

Timur did not press home his advantage: his interest lay in conquering India, so he restored power in Anatolia to Turkmen princes and allowed control of the Ottoman empire to pass to Bayezid's sons.

Left The Great Mosque in Bursa was built by Sultan Bayezid I to celebrate victory over European crusaders at Nicopolis in 1396.

Above In preparation for his attack on Constantinople, Mehmed II built a great fortress, Rumeli Hisar, to control shipping in the Bosphorus.

In 1421, Bayezid's grandson, Murad II, re-established Ottoman power over Turkmen principalities of Anatolia, forcing the Byzantine emperor to become his vassal once again. He besieged Constantinople in 1422–3, and withdrew only on payment of vast tribute.

CONQUEST

Murad's son Mehmed II laid siege to Constantinople with a vast army backed up by a fleet of 280 ships. After several weeks, in May 1453, the city fell in a matter of hours.

The conquest of Constantinople was a momentous day in the history of Islam: one of the most famous cities in the world, founded as a Greek trading colony, then re-established by Constantine as a new capital for the Roman empire and a centre of the Christian faith, was now the capital of an Islamic empire. The rapid Ottoman expansion that delivered this prize had been made possible by military might but was also powerfully driven by trade, which accrued wealth as well as necessary goods, and by religion, in particular by the activities of Sufi *tariqahs* (fraternities). The Ottomans renamed the city Istanbul and converted the Hagia Sophia and other churches into mosques.

THE CRESCENT MOON

The crescent moon and single star is an international symbol of the Islamic faith, and appears on the flags of several Muslim countries including Pakistan and Turkey. According to legend, its origin lies in a dream of Ottoman founder Osman I, in which he saw a crescent moon arching from one side of the world to the other. The Ottomans later saw in this a prophecy of their greatness.

In fact, the crescent moon and star was an ancient religious symbol in central Asia, also associated with the Greek goddess Diana. It became the symbol of the Greek colony of Byzantium, which was later transformed into the great city of Constantinople. When the Ottomans conquered Constantinople in 1453, they adopted the symbol as their own.

Left Ottoman triumph in Constantinople is depicted as the slaughter of haloed Christians in this 16th-century fresco from a Romanian monastery.

SULEYMAN THE MAGNIFICENT

THE OTTOMAN EMPIRE WAS AT ITS HEIGHT DURING THE REIGN OF SULTAN SULEYMAN 'THE MAGNIFICENT' (1520–66), WHO RULED OVER VAST TERRITORIES AND 115 MILLION PEOPLE.

The conquest of Constantinople in 1453 by Sultan Mehmed II (reigned 1451–81) was the foundation for a period of continuous Ottoman territorial expansion that brought the empire to the peak of its power and influence. Mehmed's numerous victories won him the byname of 'the Conqueror'. He captured Serbia, Bosnia, Albania and most of the territories around the Black Sea, and re-established Ottoman control in Anatolia.

His successor Bayezid II (1481–1512) consolidated these gains, with victories over Poland, Hungary and Venice. Selim I led campaigns against the Safavids of Iran and the Mamluks of Egypt, and by the end of his reign in 1520 all the territories of the old Islamic

Above Suleyman the Magnificent receives Prince Sigismund of Transylvania at his glittering court in Istanbul in this 16th-century manuscript illustration.

caliphate – aside from Iran and Mesopotamia – were now in Ottoman hands.

Suleyman I (reigned 1520–66) went even further, capturing the territory of modern Hungary from the Hapsburgs and even besieging Vienna in 1529. In the East, he won several victories over the Safavids and captured Baghdad in 1535. He extended Ottoman power all the way through Mesopotamia to the Persian Gulf, while in North Africa, he annexed Tripoli. His navy, which was commanded by the widely feared Barbarossa, dominated the eastern Mediterranean.

'THE MAGNIFICENT'
Suleyman was regarded by his contemporaries – both Christian and Muslim – as the world's

Left At the time it was built, in 1550–7, the Suleymaniye Mosque's dome was, at 53m (174ft) high, the tallest dome in the Ottoman empire.

pre-eminent ruler. Abroad, he was known as 'the Magnificent' because of the vastness of his domain and the splendour of his court. In his era, the Ottoman empire matched the Byzantine or east Roman empire in its pomp, and the extent of its territories almost exactly matched that of the eastern Roman empire under Emperor Justinian I the Great 1,000 years earlier.

Suleyman called himself 'ruler of the lands of Caesar and of Alexander the Great' and 'master of the world'. But although he promoted his own greatness, he remained devout and subject to Allah. His inscriptions also declared him to be a 'slave of Allah' and 'deputy of Allah on earth, obeying the commands of the Quran and enforcing them around the world'.

'THE LAWGIVER'

By his own people, Suleyman was called *Kanuni* ('the Lawgiver'). He revised and developed the *Kanun Nameh*, a code of imperial law first collected and promulgated by Mehmed II 'the Conqueror'. The Kanun code of law was independent of the Shariah law derived from the Quran. By tradition, Shariah law

Above Barbarossa ('Red Beard') was the scourge of western fleets in the Mediterranean for 40-odd years, first as a pirate, then as an Ottoman admiral.

Above The splendid Topkapi Palace in Istanbul was home to an imperial entourage of 4,000 people at its peak.

was applied in all Islamic states; the Ottoman Kanun law derived from the Turkish tradition, under which the law of the emperor was sacred. The code issued by Suleyman principally covered criminal law, taxation and landholding.

A number of his laws safeguarded the rights of Jews and of the *rayas* ('protected'), Christians living in their own communities within the empire. In the Ottoman empire, religious groups were permitted to set up their own communities called millets, in which they kept their own religious and other customs under their own leaders and the Sultan's protection.

In an inscription in the Suleymaniye Mosque, Suleyman was lauded as *Nashiru Kawanin al-Sultaniyye* ('Spreader of Sultanic laws'). He is traditionally viewed as the successor to the biblical King Solomon, who is praised in the Quran as the embodiment of justice. Muslims revere him as the perfect Islamic ruler.

POET AND PATRON

Suleyman was a highly cultured man. Writing under the pen name Muhibbi, he was an excellent poet, his work celebrated by Muslims as some of the finest in Islamic history. He was also a skilled goldsmith. Above all, he was a discerning and immensely generous patron of the arts. From the Topkapi Palace in Istanbul, he funded and presided over artistic societies named *Ehl-i Hiref* ('Groups of the Talented') that were a magnet for the empire's finest artists, artisans and craftsmen. During his reign, Istanbul became the artistic centre of the Islamic world, where craftsmen developed distinctively Ottoman styles.

Suleyman also embarked upon a vast building programme in Istanbul and the cities of the empire, raising bridges, palaces and mosques in great numbers. He was patron to Mimar Sinan, perhaps the greatest architect in Islam, whom he commissioned to build his first masterpiece, the beautiful Sehzade Mosque (1543–8) to honour his favourite son, Mehmed. Sinan also built the majestic Suleymaniye Mosque in Istanbul (1550–7).

From World Power to 'Sick Man of Europe'

FOLLOWING THE DEATH OF SULEYMAN I IN 1566, THE OTTOMAN EMPIRE BEGAN A LONG, VERY SLOW DECLINE THAT MADE IT, IN THE WORDS OF TSAR NICHOLAS I OF RUSSIA, THE 'SICK MAN OF EUROPE'.

For more than 100 years following Suleyman's death and the accession of Sultan Selim II in 1566, the Ottomans continued to increase their empire. However, the roots of the ultimate Ottoman decline have been traced by historians to this period.

The imperial economy was badly hit when the Dutch and British developed a sea route to Asia to replace the overland one through Ottoman lands. The economy was further damaged by inflation, partly caused by the influx of Spanish silver from 'New World' colonies in South America. A succession of weak sultans allowed decay of the previously strong administrative and military structures. The Ottoman navy was defeated by a Holy League formed by Pope Pius V and lost control of the Mediterranean. Then, during the course of the 17th

Above Under Sultan Mahmud II, the Ottoman empire began to break up as Greece won independence and Algeria was taken by the French.

century, ever more powerful nation states emerged in Europe and made alliances to curb Ottoman power.

STAGNATION AND REORDERING

Matters worsened in the 18th and early 19th centuries. The empire stagnated; many successive sultans were unsuccessful in their attempts to introduce reforms; the Ottomans failed to keep up with European developments in science, technology and military tactics. Central power waned drastically, and many areas of the empire, such as Algeria and Egypt, became effectively independent.

During the Tanzimet period (so-called from the Arabic word for 'reordering') from 1839 until 1876, Sultans Abdulmecid I and Abdulaziz

Left In the revolution of 1908–9, Young Turks fought and defeated soldiers loyal to the sultan in the streets of Istanbul.

made reforms that included the introduction of factories, an education system and a modernized army. In 1856, Abdulmecid issued the *Hatt-i Humayun* ('Imperial Reform Announcement'), which guaranteed equality for all Ottoman subjects, regardless of religious faith. Yet Ottoman power and prestige continued to fade.

LOSS OF TERRITORIES

Throughout the 19th and early 20th centuries, the Ottoman empire shrank. Nationalism was on the rise, and many former imperial territories won independence: Greece in 1829, then Montenegro, Romania and Serbia in 1878. In North Africa, Egypt was occupied by the British in 1882, while Algeria and Tunisia were colonized by the French in 1830 and 1881 respectively. During the Balkan Wars (1912–13), the empire lost all its Balkan territories except Thrace and the city of Edirne.

CONSTITUTIONAL REFORM

In 1876, Western-educated reformers named the Young Ottomans led a military coup to try to establish a constitutional monarchy. This resulted in the empire's first constitution, the *Kanun-I Esasi* ('Basic Law'), issued by Sultan Abdulhamid II in 1876. But just two years later, the sultan suspended the parliament and once again assumed absolute rule. In 1908, the revolution of the Young Turks (a coalition of reformers including secularists and nationalists) forced Abdulhamid II to restore the parliament he had suspended and reinstate the 1876 constitution.

SECULAR REPUBLIC

Following defeat in World War I, the empire was partitioned under the Treaty of Sèvres (signed in August 1920), Istanbul was occupied by

Above Mehmed Vahideddin VI was the 36th and last of the Ottoman sultans. Deposed in 1922, he died in exile in 1926 in Sanremo, Italy.

British and French troops, and a Turkish national movement mobilized to fight the Turkish War of Independence (1919–23). Mustafa Kemal led the nationalist army to victory. The Ottoman sultanate was abolished on 1 November 1922 and the last reigning sultan, Mehmed VI (reigned 1918–22) left Istanbul on 17 November. The Republic of Turkey was declared on 29 October 1923, with Mustafa Kemal as its president.

Mustafa Kemal introduced a series of secular reforms. In 1924, he abolished the Islamic caliphate and Shariah law and closed Islamic religious schools. The following year, he outlawed the wearing of

Right The memory of revolutionary leader Mustafa Kemal, the 'Father of the Turks', is celebrated in this equestrian statue in Ankara.

the fez, on the grounds that it was a symbol of the Ottoman regime, and took moves to dissuade women from wearing the veil and to encourage all to wear Western clothing. In 1926, he introduced new legal codes, under which polygamy was abolished, and religious weddings were replaced with a compulsory civil service. In 1928, he introduced a new Turkish alphabet (based on the Latin one) to replace Arabic script, and declared the state to be secular, removing the constitutional clause under which Islam was named as the official state religion. In 1933, a new law required the call to prayer and the reading of the Quran to be in Turkish rather than in Arabic.

In 1934, another law required all Turks to take Western-style surnames and the Turkish Grand National Assembly awarded Mustafa Kemal the surname Ataturk – 'Father of the Turks'.

REPUBLICS AND KINGDOMS

THE PRINCIPAL SELF-DECLARED ISLAMIC STATES ESTABLISHED IN THE 20TH CENTURY – INCLUDING PAKISTAN, SAUDI ARABIA, SUDAN, IRAN AND MOROCCO – CHOSE DIFFERENT MODELS OF GOVERNMENT.

Some Islamic states were founded as monarchies. The kingdom of Saudi Arabia (al-Mamlakah al Arabiyah as Saudiyyah), for example, is an absolute monarchy, established as a unified kingdom in 1932. The kingdom of Morocco (al-Mamlakah al Maghribiyah), which gained independence from France in 1956, is a constitutional monarchy, with a hereditary crown and a two-house parliament under a constitution agreed in 1972 and amended in 1992 and 1996.

Other states declared themselves 'Islamic republics', but this title can mean very different things. The Islamic Republic of Pakistan (*Jamhuryat Islami Pakistan*) was the first country to use the title, in its constitution of 1956. In this case, 'Islamic republic' was primarily a statement of religious and cultural identity: the constitution was a largely secular one, and Pakistan had no state religion until a revised constitution, naming Islam as the state religion, was adopted in 1973. Iran was a monarchy until the Iranian revolution of 1979, which resulted in it being declared the Islamic Republic of Iran (*Jomhuri-ye Eslami-ye Iran*). The form of government in Iran is termed a 'theocratic republic': its official religion is Shiah Islam and the chief of state or supreme leader is a Shiah imam. Its legal system is based on Shariah law.

A CALIPHATE?

Some Muslims today call for the abolition of Islamic monarchies on the grounds that they are too authoritarian. Some believe that the very notion of a republic – whether secular or Islamic – is necessarily contrary to the proper form of government as established by the Quran and Islamic tradition of the sunnah. Government, according to this theory, should be by a caliph as religious leader and successor of the Prophet, basing governance on Shariah law and Islamic religious tradition. Some call for the re-establishment of an international caliphate uniting disparate Islamic countries under religious rule. Sunni Muslims hold that when a state is ruled according to Shariah law, then this is, in fact, caliphate government in practice, whether or not the leader uses the title 'caliph'.

HISTORICAL PERSPECTIVE

The great Islamic empires were ruled by caliphs: the first four, or *Rashidun*, caliphs, the Umayyads, the Abbasids, and the Ottomans. The

Above The 12th-century Hassan Tower stands amid the ruins of an unfinished mosque in Rabat, the capital of the kingdom of Morocco.

Ottomans initially took the title *bey* (a Turkish tribal name for a ruler), then sultan and only began to use the title caliph from the reign of Selim I (reigned 1512–20) onward. When Selim defeated the Mamluk Sultanate in Egypt in 1517, the final Abbasid caliph, al-Mutawakkil III, was carried off to Istanbul; al-Mutawakkil was permitted to rule

Above Zulfikar Ali Bhutto was President of Pakistan in 1973 when a new constitution declared Islam to be the state religion of the country.

Above The Republic of Sudan, in north-eastern Africa, has been mostly ruled by military Islamic governments since its independence from Britain in 1956.

RELIGION AND SECULARISM IN TURKEY

The country created from the heartland of the great Ottoman empire, the Republic of Turkey (*Türkiye Cumhuriyeti*) has a secular constitution. There is no state religion, although Islam is a dominant force. Ninety-nine per cent of the Turkish population is Muslim, 75 per cent of these being Sunni Muslims, and around 20 per cent Alevi Muslims. (Alevis have links both to Shiah Islam and to Sufism.)

Individuals in Turkey have freedom of religion guaranteed in the constitution. Religious communities are not permitted to establish faith schools or form religious parties and no political party can claim that it represents a particular form of religion.

until his death, whereupon the title of caliph was attached to the Ottoman sultanate. Following the removal of the last Ottoman sultan Mehmed VI Vahideddin (reigned 1918–22) and the declaration of the Republic of Turkey, the first President of the Turkish Republic Mustafa Kemal abolished the caliphate as an institution in 1924.

SELF-PROCLAIMED CALIPHS

In the wake of Ataturk's decree, various individuals tried to proclaim themselves caliph. Hussein bin Ali, Sharif of Makkah and self-appointed King of the Hijaz, declared himself caliph of all Muslims just two days after Ataturk's statement. However, few paid attention to his claim and he was in any case forced to abdicate later the same year by Ibn Saud, subsequently the first King of Saudi Arabia. Mehmed VI Vahideddin, the deposed Ottoman sultan, himself attempted to declare himself caliph in the Hijaz but this also came to nothing.

The kings of Morocco and Mullah Muhammad Omar, leader of the Taliban regime of Afghanistan in the 1990s, later gave themselves the title of *amir al-mumineen* ('Commander of the Faithful') that was associated with caliphs from the 7th century onward. However, none of them claimed international jurisdiction over all Muslims, choosing to limit their power to those within their borders.

Below Built in 1971, the Shahyad Tower ('Memorial of Kings') in Tehran, Iran, was renamed Azadi ('Freedom') Tower in the 1979 Iranian Revolution.

THE MUWAHIDDUN MOVEMENT

THE REFORMIST MOVEMENT IN ISLAM THAT STRESSES *TAWHID* (THE UNITY AND UNIQUENESS OF ALLAH), WAHHABISM HAS BEEN A NOTABLE FORCE IN THE MUSLIM WORLD SINCE THE 18TH CENTURY.

Followers of scholar and religious reformer Muhammad ibn Abd al-Wahhab (1703–92) were given the name Wahhabi (*Wahhabiyyah*) by their opponents. For this reason, they reject it, preferring to be known as 'unitarians' (Muwahiddun) because of their emphasis on the oneness of Allah. This is the predominant form of Islam in Saudi Arabia and Qatar.

MUWAHIDDUN BELIEF
Muwahiddun believe that Islam should be practised as it was in the first three generations after the death of the Prophet Muhammad in 632, as revealed in the Quran and the hadith, and they reject later innovations (bidha). They denounce traditions such as venerating Islamic 'saints' and visiting the tombs of former religious leaders as idolatry, and declaim against the practice of *Tawakkul* ('drawing near to Allah'), which, in the religious practice of some Sufi, other Sunni and Twelver Shiah Muslims, involves praying to Allah through intercession to a prophet, imam or scholar.

Muwahiddun theology is largely based on the teachings of medieval Sunni Islamic scholar Taqi ad-Din Ahmad ibn Taymiyyah (1263–1328), who called for a return in Islam to following its sources in the Quran and sunnah. Its jurisprudence

Above The defenders of the first Saudi state fought bravely but were overcome by an army led by Muhammad Ali Pasha, Viceroy of Egypt, in 1818.

Below At al-Diriya (today on the outskirts of Riyadh), Muhammad ibn Saud and Ibn Abd al-Wahhab became allies. The town was capital of the first Saudi state in 1744–1818.

Left Ibn Saud, first ruler of the Kingdom of Saudi Arabia, spent most of his teenage years in exile in Kuwait after the rival Al-Rashid clan seized his ancestral lands.

is derived from the school of Ahmad ibn Hanbal (780–855), Persian Sunni Muslim scholar and theologian. Muwahiddun hold that a Muslim state should be governed solely according to Shariah Islamic law.

The Muwahiddun movement is identified by some as a form of the Sunni Islamic tradition of Salafiyyism, which draws on the actions and speeches of the Salaf (ancestors in the era of the Prophet Muhammad). The word *salaf* goes back at least until 1166, when Abu Sa'd Abd al-Kareem al-Samani wrote of '*al-Salaf* as exemplars for Muslims in his book *Al-Ansab*. Some trace the phrase to the Prophet himself, who, according to hadith, said 'I am the best *salaf* for you'. For all the possible connections to Salafiyyism, however, Abd al-Wahhab himself condemned over-reliance on scholarly tradition and stressed the capacity of the individual to discern Allah's will.

BIRTH OF THE MOVEMENT
Muhammad ibn Abd al-Wahhab established his movement in his birthplace of al-Uyayna, a village

north-west of Riyadh in Saudi Arabia, in *c*.1740. He led his followers in a number of public actions that expressed their puritan reforming zeal, including ordering the stoning of an adulteress and levelling the grave of Zayd ibn al-Khattab, brother of Caliph Umar (reigned 634–44) and one of the *sahabah* ('Companions of the Prophet'). This provoked the ire of local ruler Sulaiman ibn Muhammad ibn Ghurayr, who ordered Ibn Abd al-Wahhab to leave al-Uyayna.

Exiled in the nearby town of al-Diriya, Ibn Abd al-Wahhab won the support of its ruler, Muhammad ibn Saud, an event that would have enormous consequences over the following centuries. Ibn Abd al-Wahhab agreed to make Ibn Saud and his family the temporal leaders of his movement on condition that the Saud family would implement his teachings when they established themselves in power.

SAUDI CAMPAIGNS
Over the next 150 years or so, Ibn Saud and his heirs mounted a long succession of military campaigns to win power in the Arabian Peninsula. These campaigns brought the Saudi Wahhabis into violent conflict with other Muslims, driven particularly by their strong opposition to the practice of revering the tombs of early Muslim figures. In 1801–2, for instance, Wahhabis commanded by Abd al-Aziz ibn Muhammad ibn Saud attacked the Shiah cities of

Najaf and Karbala in Iraq, where they violated the tombs of Muhammad's son-in-law, Ali ibn Abu Talib, and grandson, Hussain ibn Ali, both of which were (and are) revered by Shiah Muslims.

Their military campaigns created what historians call the first Saudi state. The Ottoman empire, which derived prestige and authority in the Muslim world through its possession of the holy cities of Makkah and Madinah, sent troops under Muhammad Ali Pasha, Viceroy of Egypt, and he regained control of the region in 1818. A second Saudi state was created in 1824, but was brought down in 1891 by rival Arab clans. Finally, the long campaigns of the House of Saud culminated in the establishment of the Kingdom of Saudi Arabia by Abd al-Aziz ibn Saud, a direct descendant of Muhammad ibn Saud, in 1932. King Abd al-Aziz ibn Saud established his territory as a Muwahiddun state.

Above As King of Saudi Arabia, Abdullah ibn Abdul al-Aziz Al Saud is ruler of a Muwahiddun state and head of the House of Saud.

THE LAND OF THE TWO HOLY SANCTUARIES

SAUDI ARABIA, BIRTHPLACE OF ISLAM, WAS ESTABLISHED IN 1932 AS AN ISLAMIC KINGDOM, GOVERNED ACCORDING TO SHARIAH LAW AND IN LINE WITH THE PRINCIPLES OF THE MUWAHIDDUN MOVEMENT.

The kingdom of Saudi Arabia (al-Mamlakah al Arabiyah as Saudiyyah) derives great status in the global Muslim community because it contains the faith's two most sacred cities in Makkah and Madinah. The Holy Mosque in Makkah and the Prophet's Mosque in Madinah are the two holiest mosques for Muslims worldwide, and as a result Saudi Arabia is referred to reverentially as 'the Land of the Two Holy Sanctuaries'.

The Saudi king's official title is 'Custodian of the Two Holy Sanctuaries': this title was first adopted by King Fahd bin Abd al-Aziz Al Saud (reigned 1982–2005), and his successor, King Abdullah ibn Abd al-Aziz Al Saud, also uses it.

The country's motto is the first *kalimah*, or statement of the Islamic faith: 'There is no God but Allah and Muhammad is his messenger'. The motto is written on the Saudi flag, in white Arabic script against a green background and above a horizontal sabre, also in white.

ABSOLUTE POWER

King Abdullah is an absolute monarch, his powers not limited by the constitution. He himself serves as prime minister, and every four years appoints those on his Council of Ministers and the principal legislative body, the Consultative Council (*Majlis al-Shura*). In 2005, however, elections were held for half the members of 179 local assemblies, and further elections are to provide one-third of the members of the Consultative Council.

The Basic Law of Saudi Arabia, also known as the Basic System of Governance, was issued by royal decree by King Fahd in January 1992. It is based on Shariah law: limited secular legal codes have also been introduced, but these do not override Islamic laws.

Left Muslim pilgrims making the Hajj *reach up to touch the* Black Stone and door of the Kaabah *within the Holy Mosque in Makkah.*

Above The kalimah – 'There is no God but Allah and Muhammad is his messenger' – is the central feature of the flag of the kingdom of Saudi Arabia.

CREATION OF THE KINGDOM

The kingdom was established by Abdullah's father, Abd al-Aziz ibn Saud in 1902. Ibn Saud first captured the city of Riyadh, ancestral base of the Saud family, from the rival al-Rashid clan in a daring night raid on 15 January 1902. Over the following two years, he took large parts of the Nejd, the interior Arabian highlands that had been the basis of earlier states governed by the Saud dynasty in the 19th century. However, his cause suffered a major setback when, following an appeal from Ibn Rashid, leader of the al-Rashid clan, Ottoman troops marched into the region and defeated the Saudis decisively in June 1904.

Ibn Saud relaunched his campaign of expansion in 1912. During World War I, he gained British financial backing and military supplies to help in an attack on Ibn Rashid, on the grounds that the al-Rashid clan were allies of the Ottomans, and in 1922, he finally conquered all Rashidi territories. Then, in 1925, Ibn Saud captured the Hijaz, the long territorial strip along the eastern bank of the Red Sea that contains Makkah and Madinah. Ibn Saud was declared King of the Hijaz in the Great Mosque at Makkah on 10 January 1926, and the following year, under the Treaty of Jeddah, the

Above *The Prophet's Mosque in Madinah contains the tombs of Muhammad and of early caliphs Abu Bakr and Umar.*

British recognized the independence of his realm as the kingdom of the Nejd and the Hijaz.

Finally, in 1932, Ibn Saud renamed his unified realm the kingdom of Saudi Arabia. The new country comprised the regions of the Hijaz and the Nejd plus al-Qatif and al-Hasa (two oasis regions in eastern Saudi Arabia).

OIL AND RELIGIOUS FUNDING

In March 1938, vast reserves of oil were discovered in Saudi Arabia, and following World War II – in which the new county remained neutral – development began. By 1949, oil production was under way on a large scale. Saudi Arabia became the world's largest exporter of petroleum and grew very wealthy

on the proceeds. Particularly after the sharp rise in the price of oil in the mid-1970s, the Saudi government reputedly spent lavishly around the world promoting Islam.

After Iraq invaded Kuwait in 1990, Saudi Arabia accepted the exiled Kuwaiti royal family and 400,000 Kuwaiti refugees, and then, in 1991, allowed US and Arab troops to deploy on its soil prior to

attempting the liberation of Kuwait. The fact that US troops remained on Saudi soil following the liberation of Kuwait in 1991 caused rising domestic tension until the final US troops left in 2003.

Below *Scores of pilgrims take part in noon prayer (dhuhr) outside the al-Masjid al-Haram Mosque (Holy Mosque) in Makkah during the Hajj.*

AN ISLAMIC REPUBLIC

AS THE END OF BRITISH RULE IN INDIA NEARED, THE MUSLIM LEAGUE SUCCESSFULLY CAMPAIGNED TO ESTABLISH MUSLIM-MAJORITY PAKISTAN. IT WAS DECLARED AN ISLAMIC REPUBLIC IN 1956.

The modern state of Pakistan was formed on 15 August 1947. British rule ended and the Indian subcontinent was partitioned into Hindu-majority India and Muslim-majority East and West Pakistan. Both Pakistan and India were initially dominions within the Commonwealth of Nations. India became a republic on 26 January 1950 and Pakistan was declared an Islamic republic on 23 March 1956.

THE CAMPAIGN FOR INDEPENDENCE

Within India, the Muslim League led by Allama Iqbal campaigned for an independent state in north-western India for Indian Muslims from 1930 onward. In 1933, Indian Muslim nationalist Choudhary Rahmat Ali put forward the name 'Pakistan' for the proposed country. In 1940, the Muslim League adopted the Lahore Resolution, which called for the establishment of 'autonomous and sovereign' states in those parts of north-western and north-eastern India where Muslims were numerically in a majority.

In June 1947, Muhammad Ali Jinnah, as representative of the Muslim League, agreed at a meeting with representatives of the Hindu Indian National Congress, the Sikhs and the Untouchables to the creation of Pakistan. The new country of West Pakistan comprised the provinces of Baluchistan, Northwest Frontier Province, Sindh and West Punjab; meanwhile, in the north-eastern corner of the subcontinent, the province of East Bengal formed East Pakistan.

Above In September 1947, Muslims wait to leave India in a protected convoy bound for the new country of Pakistan.

VIOLENT BIRTH

The decision to split the provinces of Punjab and Bengal was highly controversial and led to wide-scale rioting and as many as 500,000 deaths. In the Punjab, millions of Muslims migrated eastward into Pakistan, while millions more Sikhs and Hindus migrated westward into India; a similar cross-border migration took place in Bengal. In total, around 14 million people were forced to relocate.

Disputes arose over the princely states, which theoretically were free to remain independent or to join either India or Pakistan. Of enduring consequence was the disagreement over Kashmir, whose Hindu ruler chose to join India, despite having a Muslim majority population; this led to a long-running dispute between India and Pakistan over the territory. The countries fought two wars – in 1947–8 and 1956 – without resolving the issue.

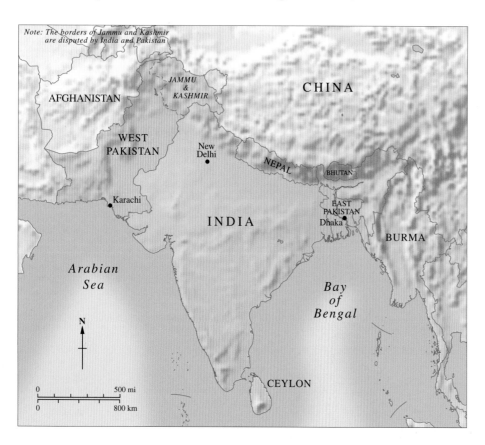

Left This map shows India with East and West Pakistan at the moment of their creation in 1947 as dominions within the Commonwealth of Nations.

CONSTITUTIONS OF PAKISTAN

Pakistan's first constitution was drawn up by the Constituent Assembly, a body established under the terms of independence from British rule in 1947. It declared the country an 'Islamic republic', provided for a parliamentary form of government and decreed that Muslims in Pakistan should be enabled to order their lives in accordance with principles in the Quran and sunnah, and that no laws 'repugnant to the injunctions of Islam' could be passed. Muslims would be required to study the Quran, and only a Muslim could be president of the country, but citizens of Pakistan would have the freedom to practise and propagate any religion they chose. It provided for parliamentary government.

In 1958, the constitution was abrogated and martial law imposed. A new constitution in 1962 renewed the majority of the above provisions; the form of government was to be presidential. Martial law continued until 1972, then a third constitution was agreed in 1973 under the rule of Zulfikar Ali Bhutto. For the first time, Islam was declared to be the state religion of Pakistan. At various times, these constitutions have been suspended and martial law imposed in Pakistan. Shariah law was introduced in the 1980s under General Muhammad Zia-ul-Haq.

THEOCRATIC RULE IN AN ISLAMIC REPUBLIC

Ayatollah Ruhollah Khomeini, Shiah Islamic scholar and an outspoken critic of the regime of the Shah of Iran, returned to Iran after 15 years of exile. Throughout his exile, he had continued to oppose the Shah's regime, and by the late 1960s, was established as a *marja-e taqlid* ('model to be imitated') by Shiah Muslims around the world. The country declared itself an Islamic Republic on 1 April 1979 and in December that year, adopted a theocratic constitution. Khomeini became Supreme Leader.

The system of government was based on the Shiah theory of *wilayat al-faqih* ('Guardianship by the Islamic Jurists'). According to this theory, Shariah laws are sufficient to cover all areas of life, and countries should be governed by a *faqih* (an expert in Shariah law). Such a system is deemed necessary to guard against oppression, injustice and corruption, and representative parliamentary systems of government are considered to be contrary to the teachings of Islam. Under the constitution of Iran, all political decisions have to be approved by the Supreme Leader before they become legal.

On Ayatollah Khomeini's death on 3 June 1989, Ayatollah Ali Khamenei became the Supreme Leader of Iran.

Right Khomeini was an ayatollah (Shiah religious leader) from the 1950s, and was in his late 70s by the time he became Supreme Leader of Iran in 1979.

RADICAL ISLAMISM

IN THE 20TH CENTURY, WHILE MANY MUSLIM GROUPS ENCOURAGED MODERNIZATION, SOME ISLAMIC ACTIVISTS URGED RADICAL POLITICAL OR TERRORIST ACTION TO REFORM SOCIETY AND GOVERNMENT.

Above Shaykh Ahmad Yassin was co-founder, with Abdel Aziz al-Rantissi, of the militant Islamist organization Hamas in the Palestinian Territories in 1987.

Several groups over the course of the 20th century called for a revival of Islam through a return to the faith's central tenets and most ancient traditions. Writers and teachers proposed that Islam was more than a religion, and that social and political systems should be remade according to the faith. This theory was generally called *al-Islamiyyah* ('Islamism').

THE MUSLIM BROTHERHOOD

The Muslim Brotherhood, or the Society of the Muslim Brothers (*al-Ikhwan al-Muslimun*) was established in Egypt in 1928 to promote a return to the Quran and sunnah as the basis for modern Islamic societies. The Brotherhood spread quickly to Palestine, the Lebanon, Syria, the Sudan and North Africa.

In the late 1930s and 1940s, the Muslim Brotherhood became politicized, and in Egypt in 1952, it supported the coup led by Gamal Abdel Nasser, whom they expected to found an Islamic religious government. Disappointed by his development of secular nationalism, the Brotherhood attempted to assassinate him in 1954.

One of the leading figures of the movement in the 1950s and 1960s was the Egyptian intellectual Sayyid Qutb. While in prison for his involvement in the planning of the failed assassination (he was later hanged), he wrote a strongly anti-Western and anti-secular book

Below Mujahidun are those who struggle in jihad – in opposition to qaid, a person who does not join jihad. These mujahidun were fighting in Afghanistan.

Ma'alim fi-l-Tariq (*Milestones*). In this influential book, Qutb denounced all existing governments, even those of the Muslim countries, as subject to *jahiliyyah* (ignorance). He appealed to Muslims to form a revolutionary vanguard that would

oppose *jahiliyyah* through preaching and by removing governmental systems that supported *jahiliyyah*, through 'physical power and *jihad*'.

HAMAS

In the Palestinian Territories, members of the Gaza wing of the Muslim Brotherhood founded Hamas, the *Harakat-al-muqawamah al-islamiyyah* ('Islamic Resistance Movement') in 1987. The organization is associated with suicide bombings and other attacks on the Israeli military and on civilians; its founding charter called for the state of Israel to be destroyed and replaced with an Islamic state. Hamas is also a political party and won a majority of seats in the elected council of the Palestinian Authority in Gaza in January 2006.

AL-QAEEDA

Qutb's writings were a direct influence on the international Islamic *jihad* movement of al-Qaeeda, which was behind the terrorist attacks on New York City and Washington on 11 September 2001, and subsequently became one of the central targets of the United States' 'war on terror'. Qutb's brother, Muhammad Qutb, became a professor of Islamic studies and

Above A propaganda billboard in the Lebanese capital Beirut promotes the armed struggle of the Shiah militia Hezbollah in the Lebanon.

promoted Qutb's theories. One of his students was Ayman al-Zawahiri, who was reputedly a mentor of al-Qaeeda leader Osama bin Laden and eventually a leading member of al-Qaeeda himself.

There is considerable debate over what al-Qaeeda actually is. Its name perhaps means the 'base' and, according to some accounts, it grew out of the organization set up to train *mujahidun* (Muslims fighting *jihad*) fighting against the Afghan Marxist regime and Soviet troops in Afghanistan in the 1980s.

In 1998, its emerging leader, Osama bin Laden, and Ayman al-Zawahiri issued a *fatwa* calling on Muslims to expel foreign troops and interests from Islamic lands, to 'fight the pagans…until there is no more tumult or oppression…and there prevail justice and faith in Allah'.

Many writers suggest that although training camps in Sudan and Afghanistan were reputedly run under its aegis, al-Qaeeda is not actually a centralized organization, but is, in fact, a loose-knit group of Islamists dedicated to *jihad*.

Above Osama bin Laden, alleged founder of al-Qaeeda, ranked Shiah Muslims alongside heretics, the US and Israel as the four main 'enemies of Islam'.

GLOSSARY

ADHAN the call to prayer signalling the congregational times of the five daily prayers. *See also muadhdhin.*

ADL justice, equity or equality.

AHL AL-BAYT 'the people of the house', the immediate family of the Prophet, namely Muhammad, Fatimah, Ali, Hassan and Hussain. Significant in Shiah theology.

AHL AL-DHIMMAH religious minorities living under Muslim rule.

AHWAL (singular *hal*) the different temporary states of spirituality experienced through Sufi practice.

AKHLAQ morality and ethics. In its singular form, the word means character, manners and etiquette.

AL-*BURAQ* the winged, horselike beast that Muslims believe carried Muhammad to Jerusalem and then to heaven on the *Isra* and *Miraj.*

AL-*DAJJAL* the Antichrist who it is said will appear before the end of times, wreak havoc on earth and be killed by Jesus after his second coming.

AL-*GHAYB* the unseen world; a created reality but not seen with the human eye (for example, *jinn,* or heaven).

AL-*MAHDI* literally 'the guided one', a descendant of the Prophet Muhammad, who Muslims believe will appear at the end of time and establish peace on earth. In Shiah theology, he is the 12th awaited imam, the 'hidden imam'.

AL-*MASIH* literally 'the anointed one', referring to Jesus.

AL-*MUHADDITHUN* scholars of hadith and Islamic jurists.

AL-*SIRAH AL-NABAWIYYAH* biographical accounts of the Prophet's life.

AL-*YAWM AL-AKHIR* the Last Day or Day of Judgement.

AMIR the leader of a Muslim community.

AQD a legal contract or agreement.

ARAFAH the valley plain near Makkah where *Hajj* pilgrims spend the day in repentance and prayer.

ASR the third prayer of the day, offered in late afternoon.

AYAH a verse from the Quran.

BATIN the hidden or esoteric.

BURQA a long overgarment, usually black, covering the entire body of a Muslim woman. Also usually covers face with a veil. *See also niqab.*

CALIPH the appointed leader of the Muslim community in early Islamic history until the Ottoman times.

DHAHIR the manifest and known, or the physical and tangible world.

DHIKR remembrance of God through spiritual practices of repeating his name and praises.

DHUHR the second prayer of the day, offered early in the afternoon.

DIN religion, a way of life.

DUNYA earthly existence.

EID the celebration at the end of Ramadhan (*Eid ul-fitr*) and *Hajj* (*Eid ul-adha*).

ESCHATOLOGY branch of theology concerning the final events in the history of the world or humankind.

FAJR the first prayer of the day, offered just before sunrise.

FAQIH (plural *fuqaha*) a Muslim scholar of Islamic religious law.

FARD an obligatory action that must be performed by every sane, healthy adult.

FATWA a religious edict; a legal opinion, issued by a *mufti* (legal expert), although it is not binding in nature.

FIQH body of jurisprudential principles derived from Shariah by legal scholars exercising their understanding of the law.

FITRA the state of natural or primordial disposition.

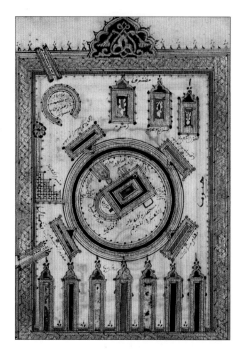

Above *An 18th-century plan of the Sacred Mosque in Makkah. Muslims believe that the original mosque was built by Ibrahim and Ismail.*

FURQAN 'the criterion', referring to the Quran as the measure of what is right and wrong.

GHULUW excessiveness, extremism.

GHUSL ritual bath to attain purification, a state that is compulsory before offering prayers.

HADITH the sayings and narrations of the Prophet.

HAJJ pilgrimage to the *Kaabah* in Makkah: the fifth pillar of Islam.

HANIF (plural *hunafa*) a believer in one God but without any professed or formal religion.

HARAM actions that are forbidden/unlawful under Islamic law.

HIJAB a headscarf worn by women to cover all the hair.

HIJRAH the Prophet Muhammad's migration from Makkah to Madinah in 622CE.

IBADAH (plural *ibadat*) an act of worship. This forms the 'personal' part of Islamic law.

IFTAR the meal taken at sunset to break the fast during Ramadhan.

IHRAM the simple two-piece (usually) white cloth worn by pilgrims on *Hajj*.

IJMA the majority consensus of Muslim scholars.

IJTIHAD exerted effort by the use of analogy to arrive at an Islamic legal opinion.

IMAM In Shiah theology, the leader of the Muslim community from the descendants of the Prophet. In Sunni practice, the religious leader of the mosque community.

ISHA the fifth prayer of the day, offered at nightfall.

ISLAM as a verb, wilful submission to God; peace. As a noun, the faith of Islam as taught by the Prophet Muhammad.

ISNAD the chain of hadith transmitters connecting directly to the Prophet Muhammad.

ISRA the Prophet's night journey with Archangel Jibril to Jersualem from Makkah on al-Buraq.

JAHANNAM hellfire.

JAHILIYYAH ignorance; a term used to described the state of polytheist pre-Islamic Arabia.

JIHAD (verb) to struggle. Usually refers to the 'greater' self-struggle of purifying the soul from earthly desires, but also means physical/ military struggle (which is known as the 'lesser' *jihad*).

JINN creatures of the unseen who, like humans, have been endowed with free will.

JIZYAH the exemption tax paid by religious minorities under Muslim rule.

JUMUAH Friday, the day of congregational prayer.

JUZ (plural *ajza*) one portion of the Quran divided into 30 parts.

KAABAH the cubelike edifice in the Haram Mosque, Makkah, which is considered to be the first house of worship.

KAFIR (plural *kuffar*) a theological definition of a non-believer.

KALAM the rhetorical expositions of philosophers.

KUFR disbelief.

LIAN a particular oath relating to alleged infidelity and taken in a divorce petition.

MADHHAB Islamic jurisprudential school or developed method of legal interpretation.

MADINAH the city of Yathrib, which became known as 'the city of the Prophet'.

MADRASA a school/seminary/ college/class for learning the Quran and Islam, usually attached to a mosque.

MAGHRIB the fourth compulsory prayer of the day at sunset.

Right *A battle scene from the* Suleymanname, *an illustrated history of the life of Suleyman the Magnificent, dating from the 16th century.*

Above Now a Christian church, the Mezquita of Córdoba was originally built by Abd al-Rahman I in 784 and remained a mosque until 1236.

MAKKAH Muhammad's birth city and the place of Ibrahim's ancient temple, the *Kaabah*.

MALAK (plural *malaaikah*) an angel.

MAQAM (plural *maqamat*) different stations on the Sufi path that are experienced on the journey toward God (for example, repentance and gratitude).

MAQASID established principles or reasons for Islamic rulings and interpretations.

MATN used in relation to hadith interpretation, meaning the hadith's content or principle.

MAWLID the Prophet's birthday celebration; also known as *Milad*.

MIHRAB arched niche in the mosque from where the imam leads congregational prayers.

MINBAR pulpit to the right of the *mihrab* with a flight of stairs leading to the top, from where the imam delivers his sermons.

MIRAJ the Prophet's Night Journey to heaven, on al-Buraq. *See also Isra.*

MIZAN scales or balance.

MUADHDHIN the caller who recites the *adhan*, to call believers to the ritual prayers.

MUAMALAT those aspects of Islamic law dealing with social relations and interactions.

MUFTI an Islamic jurist qualified to give a legal ruling.

MUHARRAM the first month of the Islamic calendar, also the month in which Hussain, the Prophet's grandson, was martyred at Karbala.

MUJAHID (plural *mujahidun*) a Muslim engaged in physical *jihad*.

MURSHID a Sufi master, attached to a *tariqah* (Sufi order), who guides his/her disciples. Also known as a *shaykh*.

MUSALLAH 'a place of prayer'. Refers both to the physical place of prayer and a prayer mat.

MUSLIM one who submits his or her will to worshipping one God: a follower of the religion of Islam.

MUWAHHIDUN unitarian belief stressing the oneness of God, and used as a self-label by those more usually called 'Wahhabis' by critics. *See also* Wahhabism.

NABI a prophet of Allah.

NAFS the ego encompassing human virtues and desires.

NIKAH the marriage contract, detailing an offer by the groom, acceptance by the bride, witnessed by two people.

NIQAB face veil.

QADI an Islamic judge, who presides over legal matters and proceedings.

QADAR God's divine measure, decree or predestination.

QIBLA the direction of prayer facing toward the *Kaabah* in the city of Makkah.

QIYAM-UL-LAYL night of devotional prayer to achieve nearness to God, through either formal prayer or recitation of the Quran and *dhikr*.

QIYAS analogous reasoning used in applying Islamic jurisprudence.

QURAN the book of divine revelations that Muslims believe was revealed by God to the Prophet Muhammad via Archangel Jibril.

QURAYSH the ruling Arab tribe of Makkah during the pre-Islamic period of Muhammad's era.

RAMADHAN the ninth month of the Islamic calendar, during which Muslims fast. *See also sawm.*

RASUL God's messenger.

RIBA usury. The taking or giving of interest in economic transactions is forbidden by Islam because it is considered to be unjust.

RISALAH divine messengership. Denotes the messenger bringing a divine text, such as the Quran and Torah, to humankind.

RUH the spirit or the soul.

SALAH (plural *salawat*) formal ritual prayer, offered in Arabic, reciting verses from the Quran and other prayers, toward the direction of the *Kaabah*. Apart from the five compulsory prayers, *salah* can also be extra optional units of prayer. *Salah* is the second pillar of Islam.

SAWM fasting in the month of Ramadhan, the fourth pillar of Islam. Usually begins with *suhur* (a meal taken before sunrise).

SHAHADAH the first pillar of Islam; the declaration of faith that there is no god but the one God and that Muhammad is his prophet.

SHAYKH An elder, leader or teacher. *See also murshid.*

SHAYTAN Satan, the devil. Also known as Iblis.

SHIAH a Muslim who follows the minority political and theological system that recognizes Ali and his descendants as the rightful heirs and leaders of the Muslim community.

Above A detail of the exquisite tiling on the vaulted ceiling of the traditional Nasir al-Mulk Mosque in Shiraz, Iran, completed in 1888.

SHIRK polytheism, or the sin of associating partners with God.

SHURA consultation, or the act of seeking council by the caliph from learned advisors.

SILSILAH Sufi chain or order of spiritual authority.

SIRAH the biography or historical account of the Prophet Muhammad.

SUFISM/*TASAWWUF* mysticism, spiritual inner journey where remembrance and love of God, together with purification of the heart, is emphasized more than outer dimensions of faith.

SUNNAH the 'way' or life example of the Prophet Muhammad.

SUNNI a term used to describe the overwhelming majority of Muslims, who adhere to the teachings and life example of the Prophet.

SURAH a chapter from the Quran.

TAFSIR exegesis or explanation and interpretation of the Quran.

TAJWEED the art of reciting the Quran.

TALBIYAH 'I am at your command O Allah, I am at your command', the prayer recited by pilgrims throughout the *Hajj*.

TAQLID adherence to established Islamic legal rulings.

TAQWA an all-encompassing awareness of God.

TARAWIH the extra optional night prayer offered in congregation during Ramadhan.

TARIQAH a Sufi order of brotherhood, organized with a spiritual guide (*murshid*) helping his or her disciples (*murids*) on their inner journey to God.

TAWBAH repentance. The process of asking God for forgiveness to attain purity of faith.

TAWHID God's oneness or unicity.

TAZIYAH passion plays and models of Hussain's mosque, carried in processions to commemorate his martyrdom in Muharram.

TAZKIYAH purification of the soul. A deeply spiritual exercise.

ULAMA Islamic religious scholars.

UMMAH the universal Muslim community.

UMMATUN WASATA the Muslim nation as a community of moderation.

VICEGERENT a deputy or steward to God on earth.

WAHHABISM the name often given to the puritanical reform movement founded by Muhammad ibn Abd al-Wahhab in the 18th century, adopted by the ruling family in Saudi Arabia.

WUDU ritual ablutions to prepare for prayer.

YAWM AL-QIYAMAH the Day of Resurrection.

ZAKAH the required Islamic principle of giving alms to the poor. The third pillar of Islam.

ZAMZAM, WELL OF the well in Makkah that, according to Islam, sprang up when Ismail's mother, Hajar, searched for water in the barren valley to quench his thirst.

INDEX

Below Iznik tiles from the Circumcision Chamber of Topkapi Palace in Istanbul.

Above A late 16th-century Ottoman painting depicting Jonah and the whale.

Above Procession of a sacred camel on a pilgrimage to Makkah and Madinah.

PICTURE CREDITS